MW01288786

Work, Save, Travel, Repeat

The complete guide to amazing budget traveling

Jereme M. Lamps

DEDICATION

To my unicorn: whomever and wherever she may be

Table of Contents

Acknowledgements

I am nothing without my friends and family. I am eternally grateful for their unwavering support and encouragement throughout my endeavors.

In particular, I would like to express my deepest gratitude to Emily Schroeder, Stephanie Schneider, Katie Lamps, and Tom Finlayson. You were complete rockstars in helping me take the rough draft of my book and converting it into a finished product.

Disclaimers

I have personally used and fully endorse all the websites and products that are recommended in this book. I do not receive any money or benefit from making my recommendations; I just truly believe in what I am recommending. Readers should be aware that the websites listed in this book may change. I do not have any control over a website's content.

There is always a chance something bad can happen to you in your day-to-day life. The same is true when you travel. The information provided in this book is designed to provide helpful information on the subjects discussed. This book does not contain any guarantees, and I am not liable for any damages or negative consequences to any persons reading or following the information in this book. You are responsible for your own choices, actions, and results. Always be cautious and use your best judgement.

Throughout the book, I will use the term "Americans" and mean "people from the United States of America." I acknowledge South Americans are also Americans. I will use the simplistic generalization because of my background and because it is less wordy than saying "people from the United States of America" and less goofy sounding than something like "United Statians

Section 1: Introduction

"Travel is the only thing you buy that makes you richer" – Unknown

O ver 500 days ago, I quit my job, packed up my life, and left to explore the world. Before I embarked on this journey, my friends told me I needed to write a book detailing my adventures. Initially, I had no intention of writing a single word, but as once-in-a-lifetime experiences continued to pile up, I began to reconsider the idea. However, a book simply chronicling my adventures is NOT the vision I had for my writing. Instead, the sole purpose of this book is to inspire. To inspire the person that had never considered traveling to faraway destinations, or the person that had pondered it but never considered it possible, or the person that yearns with all their heart to travel but simply doesn't know where to start—these are the people I hope this book can reach. My 500 day journey has given me my fair share of incredible experiences, and with the knowledge I've gained with these experiences, I hope to help other people go out, explore the world, and collect their own fantastic and unforgettable stories. Not only that, but I firmly believe the world would be a better place if more people traveled more frequently. As people travel, they inevitably begin to learn about other cultures, religions, and ideas. In turn, they will continue to grow and expand their minds, frequently becoming more tolerant, knowledgeable, and accepting.

One thing I noticed during my journey is that I did not meet many Americans who were traveling for long periods of time. When I did meet Americans, they would usually only be traveling for a week or two. Instead, I would meet loads of French and Australians taking these epic journeys for months at a time. For example, I met an amazing French couple who had bought horses and were riding around central Asia on horseback! How epic is that?

So I wanted to investigate this further. Why does it seem like people from certain countries travel for longer periods of times than others? After talking with friends from different parts of the world who had not traveled much before, it seemed there were two main obstacles deterring worldwide travel: the cost of traveling and the fear/anxiety/stress of traveling (especially while solo). This book will tackle both of these 'deterrents' head-on. Not only will you discover that travel can be inexpensive and not so scary, but you will also learn that traveling cheaply is the best way to explore the world. Think of this book as a complete guide to budget traveling. After you have finished reading, you should realize you can travel economically, as well as be prepared for any situation that may arise once you begin your own incredible journey.

The other objective I had while writing this book was to keep it as short as possible. A lot of the budget travel books I read before writing this one were *long*. I was forced to invest lots of time into each book, and I did not like that— I just wanted to travel! For the sake of brevity, my target for this book was to keep it around 150 pages. Rather than inundate you with a bunch of fluffy and flowery bullshit, I will present the pertinent information, along with some fun and personal experiences to drive points home.

But before we dive in, just a little bit about me. I come from a middle-class family and was raised in rural Illinois, about 1.5 hours from Chicago. With my mom working as a part-time nurse and my dad as a full-time farmer/engineer, we always had enough money for food on the table, but not enough for my little brother and I to ever get separate bedrooms. Yup, that's right - I was stuck on the top bunk of the bunk bed until I moved away to college. Later on, my parents would take the stance that they were simply helping me practice for hostel dorm life, but, of course, that was not the reason. In reality, our family did not have enough money to move into a larger house which would allow each of my three siblings and I to get our own room. Later, when planning for college, I was put into the same situation nearly all other college students and their families face nowadays: figuring out how to pay for an expensive college education. Armed with the hard truth that my parents would not be able to support me, I used the little money I had saved up from high school jobs, applied for dozens of scholarships, and, inevitably, took out student loans. To cut overall costs, I spent my first year at a community college, lived in small apartments with many roommates, and overloaded my schedules at university, which enabled me to graduate a semester early with a Computer Science degree. Upon graduation, I was blessed to be offered a good programming job, which I immediately accepted and entered the workforce. For the next five years, I lived very frugally while I worked at the same job, paid off my student loans, saved money for the future, and discovered what I was truly passionate about: traveling.

I was 23 when I had saved up enough vacation time and money for my first international trip. Before 23, I had never been abroad before, not even to Mexico or Canada. So I did as any sensible young man would do and booked a flight pretty much as far away from the United States as possible: Thailand. Go big or go home, right? Well, I can safely say it was one of the best decisions of my life. After overcoming the initial culture shock of arriving in a completely exotic and foreign land, I quickly fell in love. I mean, what is there not to love about the abundance of breathtaking beaches, insanely delicious Pad Thai, and ridiculously cheap alcohol? Mix all of that together, combined with all of the amazing people I met, and it makes for an incredible first international experience. I had officially been bitten by the infamous travel bug.

For the next four years, any vacation time earned or extra cash saved from work went towards my next international trip. Every experience to a new country satiated my desire to travel for a little while, but it was never enough. I think some of this can be attributed to the slight tinge of jealousy I would feel when meeting other international travelers. I would meet extremely interesting people who have been traveling for 6, 8, or 10+ months (usually Australians, they seem to travel indefinitely!) who regaled me with stories from their lengthy journeys. Eventually, when they asked me how long I had been traveling, I always felt silly because my answer was usually in the 6-10 days range. I soon realized that 6-10 days per trip was simply not enough time to experience all that I wanted to see and do. So, with this burning desire to travel always present in the back of my mind, I would continue to live frugally and save money wherever I could. At 27, with this fire still raging and a decent amount of money in my savings account, I built up the confidence to quit my job, and embarked on a 500-day journey across the world that would change my view on life forever.

This book is ordered as follows:

Section 2 discusses "Traveling on a Budget" and presents all of the various tips and tricks I have learned on how to travel cheaply.

Section 3 discusses "Issues While Traveling" and talks about all of the various physical, emotional, or technical problems that can arise while traveling and how to overcome them.

Section 4 is "Lessons Learned," where I talk about the biggest life lessons I learned while traveling for the last 500 days.

Section 5 is the conclusion, and after the conclusion I have included an Appendix that contains a well-defined list of all essential travel items as well as incredible travel apps I have personally used during my journey.

Throughout the book I have sprinkled in personal anecdotes to either reinforce a concept or dissuade you from making a similar mistake.

So what are you waiting for? Let's get started!

Section 2: Traveling on a budget

"You don't have to be rich to travel well. " – *Eugene Fodor*

Most of us love the idea of relaxing on exotic beaches, hiking breathtaking mountains, or gorging on delicious new foods. Many also think traveling is something that is expensive to the point of being prohibitive. But it does not have to be that way! Sure, you can stay in the 5-star resorts and easily spend lots of money in short periods of time, but I would argue it is not the best way to travel if you want to experience new cultures in their raw and unfiltered form. In actuality, you can travel to many places incredibly cheaply as long as you know all the tricks to budget traveling. I would consider myself a moderate budget traveler. Throughout my journey I met people who I would consider ultra-budget travelers. For example, I met a guy named Josh who spent 338 days literally walking from Azerbaijan to Tajikistan. In total he walked 3400 kilometers (2100 miles) and would always sleep outside unless someone offered him a place to sleep for free. When he cooked, he would only eat plain white rice and the cheapest cookies money could buy. Incredibly, he spent $405 over 338 days, or $1.20 a day! Josh's cost-saving methods are truly impressive, but I think only a few select people could do some of the extreme things that he did. It takes a special person to live at that daily budget, and much of the time it must have been incredibly arduous and grueling. This type of ultra-budget travel is not for me. I prefer to eat out at local restaurants, know where I am going to sleep, drink beer, and visit the occasional tourist attractions. This section will explore all the latest and greatest technologies and techniques I have used in order to save money and maximize the overall trip experience. You will not have to travel in such an extreme way as my friend Josh did, but you will still be able to travel extremely cheap! The biggest expenses during traveling are transportation, accommodation, and miscellaneous (food, laundry, etc), so they will be broken up accordingly.

Section 2.1: Cheap flights

For me, flying always seemed to be the biggest expense of any trip. Luckily, there are a couple services I discovered that significantly reduce the cost of flying while traveling: ScottsCheapFlights and SkyScanner.

ScottsCheapFlights

ScottsCheapFlights is a subscription service you can sign up for that will email you amazing flight deals as they are discovered. This is an amazing service if you are pretty flexible on dates and destinations. If you subscribe to this service, oftentimes you will see flights at over a 50% discount! Here is an example of an email I received from ScottsCheapFlights:

NORMAL PRICE: $900+ roundtrip

TO **Barcelona** BCN 🇪🇸 Spain

FROM	ROUNDTRIP
Cleveland CLE	**$492**
Phoenix PHX	**$488**
Portland PDX	**$489**
Tampa TPA	**$469**

BOOK BY

We think this deal will last 1-2 days

TRAVEL DATES

Varies by route. Generally January through early April and October through mid-November 2020. Some routes have additional availability April through June and August through September for around $50 more roundtrip

AIRLINES

Iberia (oneworld)   Delta (SkyTeam)
KLM (SkyTeam)

As you can see, the email contains a wealth of information. At the top, the very first thing you see is the regular price for the flight. Knowing the regular price can give you an idea of how much money you are saving. Then it tells you the destination country as well as departure cities that are applicable with this deal at the very low price. Further down it will tell you what months you can find this deal, the airlines that are offering these cheap flights, and how long the service predicts these flights will be available. In this example, if you were to fly out of Tampa, you would save $431 from what you would normally pay! To fully utilize this service, you need to be quick, as time is of the essence. There have been cases where I tried to purchase a cheap flight a day or two after I received the email, but it was too late, and the tickets were regular price again. Finally, at the bottom of the email is a link you can click titled "Sample Google Flights Search" which will take you directly to Google Flights, demonstrating the deal. From there you can mess around with the city and dates to get it to match up with something that works for your schedule. ScottsCheapFlights also offers a "Premium Membership" for $49 a year. This Premium Membership will give you the best possible deals the service finds. I do not know if the extra membership is worth it on your own, but it definitely is if you can get a couple of your friends together to split the cost.

As I mentioned before, this service is amazing if you can be flexible. A few years back, when I was living in Albuquerque, some friends and I wanted to go to Germany for Oktoberfest. Unfortunately, tickets from Albuquerque to Germany were $1200+ and way more than what I was able to spend on a flight. A few weeks later, I saw a ScottsCheapFlights deal from Los Angeles to Spain for only $237 round trip! I knew flying from Albuquerque to Los Angeles was cheap, as was flying around Europe (once you are in Europe!), so I booked the flight immediately. A roundtrip between Albuquerque and Los Angeles ended up costing $160, and a roundtrip between Spain and Germany costing $60. When it was all said and done, the total flying cost for my Oktoberfest trip was $457, significantly less than the $1200+ I would have spent if I had not used ScottsCheapFlights.

SkyScanner

Another service I am constantly using is called SkyScanner. It is a website that allows you to make interesting queries to find the absolute cheapest flight option. SkyScanner has so many cool searches I will not be able to talk about them all, but here are examples of two of my most common ones:

I want to leave New York City on November 14th and go anywhere, where can I go?

This will return the cheapest places you can get to from New York City on the specified date and can be done by putting the word "Everywhere" in the destination location. From there, simply click on the country that interests you for more information.

From	To	Depart	Return
NYC (Any)	Everywhere	14/11/2019	(One Way)
Direct flights only			

Estimated lowest prices only. Found in the last 8 days.

United States		from $46	∨
Canada		from $69	∨
Bermuda		from $87	∨
Cayman Islands		from $119	∨
Dominican Republic		from $122	∨

With this exact search, I was able to find a direct flight to Santo Domingo in the Dominican Republic for only $122!

I want to travel from Miami to Paris in November 2019, what are the cheapest days to travel?

This will return the cheapest prices from Miami to Paris for each day in November, and present it in a graph so you can quickly determine which days are the cheapest to travel. Just look for the day where the cost is the smallest and select that one. For this example, if you were to fly out on November 13th you would only pay $155! This is so much cheaper than if you were naive and simply booked a flight on November 9th for $388 and not checking the price graph on SkyScanner.

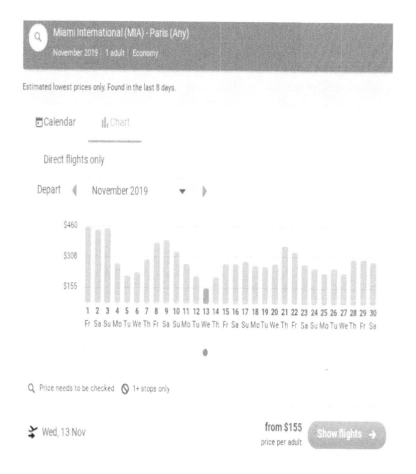

If you are a more visual person, SkyScanner also allows you to perform the same type of search but with the results overlayed on a map instead. In this example, my search was a mixture of the previous two examples. I wanted to see the cheapest places I could fly to from Budapest in the month of October. As you can see, it is presented in a beautiful way in which you can quickly see which places are cheapest to fly to. For reference, anything in green means the flight is non-stop, while circles in red will have one or more layover. Simply hover over a circle to see the price to get to that particular city. From this map, you can quickly see how cheap you can get around Europe from Budapest. You can fly non-stop to Berlin for only $31, London for only $36, or Milan for only $30!

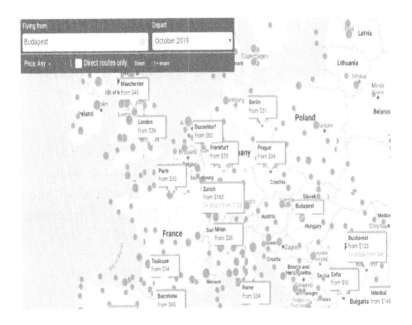

Section 2.2: Hitchhiking

At first I was not sure if I wanted to include a hitchhiking section in this book because a lot of people (especially Americans) consider it risky, difficult, and dangerous. While this may be a perception in the United States, I have found that in many cultures hitchhiking is a common practice and actually relatively safe. When I embarked on my journey, I did not have any intention of hitchhiking. That is, until I met a young Australian in Bulgaria named Stephanie who had been hitchhiking through Europe and the Middle East *for the past 2 years*. After hearing her story, I became inspired to give hitchhiking a try, and I was lucky enough for Stephanie to say she would help me get started. For the next five weeks, Stephanie and I traveled throughout Eastern Europe only by hitchhiking. During this time, we developed some general rules which will make any hitchhiking experience more reliable, safe, and enjoyable:

Try to hitchhike with one other person: If your group is too large, it is unlikely that someone will have enough space to pick everyone up. If you are alone (especially if you are a woman), it is just taking on extra risk to be hitchhiking by yourself.

Sign legibility: Make a cardboard sign that has legibly written where you want to go.

Good hitchhiking spot: Your hitchhiking spot should be on the edge of town at a gas station or an entry ramp to the highway. You need a spot where cars are going slow enough so they have enough time to read your sign, determine if you look trustworthy, and have a safe spot to stop and pick you up. If you try to hitchhike in town, a vast majority of the cars will not be heading the way you are going, plus there is usually too much traffic. There were a couple times when Stephanie and I unfortunately had to hitchhike on the highway. Not only did it feel way more dangerous because cars were zipping by us, but it took the longest amount of time on average for a vehicle to actually stop for us.

Appear respectable: This should go without saying, but if you appear presentable, you will have a better chance of getting picked up.

Take off your hat and sunglasses: You appear more trustworthy if people can see your eyes. Since you are trying to build an instantaneous level of trust with the driver, taking off anything covering your eyes will improve those chances.

Do not hitchhike in the rain: When it is raining we always seemed to make poor decisions and take rides with people we should not have.

Man in front: If you are in a man/woman team, always have the guy sit up front. This is a rule Stephanie had for our group and I think it worked really well. Oftentimes, solo guy drivers will stop to pick you up, and let's face it, sometimes guys can be creepy. Having your male teammate sit up front reduces the chances of the driver becoming a little creepy. Stephanie and I used this rule for weeks without a single problem of drivers becoming weird.

Always exclaim "No Money!": Saying this before

entering the car will ensure you and the driver have the same expectations.

◆ ◆ ◆

I am really glad I started hitchhiking on this journey for many reasons. Not only was I able to save so much money, but more times than not it was actually the fastest way for me to get around. For example, in Eastern Europe I would get picked up within 15 minutes. It was even better in Thailand or Turkey, where most of the time I would not even have to wait a minute to get picked up by a friendly driver. In addition, I met so many interesting local people hitchhiking. I do not believe I would have had a similar experience if I were taking a bus or some other form of transportation.

In all the time I spent hitchhiking, I only had two questionable experiences. You will notice, in both experiences I broke some of the rules I outlined above. If you stick to the rules I mentioned, you should be able to greatly reduce your chances of any sort of problem.

My first bad hitchhiking experience

The first questionable experience occurred when Stephanie and I were trying to get to Belgrade in Serbia. We found a driver using the techniques described above and we thought everything was going well when, unfortunately, something came up with the driver and he was unable to take us the rest of the way to Belgrade. He ended up dropping us off in the middle of the highway and turning around. Although it was a rule of ours not to hitchhike on the highway, we felt desperate because there were no large towns nearby, so we did it anyway. After 45 minutes of rejection after rejection, our spirits were getting low. To make matters worse, it was starting to rain. At this time, a bus saw us and stopped. Thank god! I shook the bus attendants' hand with a smile and sat down. I realized afterwards I had forgotten to exclaim "No Money", but I figured it was so obvious we were hitchhiking that it would be okay. When we arrived in Belgrade, we went to the front of the bus because I wanted to shake the drivers hand and thank him for his kindness. However, he would not shake my hand; instead, he looked at us sternly and demanded money. The driver and bus attendant cornered us in the bus and literally would not let us leave until we gave them something. We ended up handing over $5 and running off the bus.

Rules we broke: No hitchhiking on the highway, no hitchhiking in the rain, and always saying "No Money"

My second bad hitchhiking experience

My scariest hitchhiking experience happened when we were traveling between Albania and Kosovo. It was lightly raining as Stephanie and I were walking to the point where we wanted to start hitchhiking. While on the way there, two men in a car stopped for us and said they could take us across the border. We failed to mention "No Money," and because we did not want to be rained on any further, we hopped in the car. Everything was fine when we were crossing the border, but when we arrived at our destination and got out of the car, they started demanding money. The driver was a wiry little guy, with a sneer reminiscent of a snarling hyena. The other guy was much more intimidating, at a height of around 6'3" and a bulky frame. We tried to calmly explain to them that we were hitchhiking and did not have any money, but they continued to get angrier and angrier. The driver started pointing to his rear driver's side headlight, saying we "broke it" and that he would call the police. This was clearly a bullshit bluff. I tried to hand him all of the Albanian Lek I had left over from Albania (which is about $1.50), but the driver refused to take my money. After more arguing, I left the $1.50 on the trunk of his car and we started walking down the street towards our hostel. About two minutes later, Stephanie whispers to me to turn around, and I realize the two guys had been following us and were right behind us! When they caught up to us, they continued to yell at us in Albanian. We showed them our empty pockets, and out of nowhere the bigger guy lunged in to take a swing at me! Somehow, I managed to dodge it by knocking his hand away, gave him a little shove, and shouted "No money!" before Stephanie and I quickly ran away. Thankfully, we were quicker than they were, and after a few minutes of them trying to catch us, we were able to lose them by ducking into a smoky Italian restaurant. We sipped our cappuccinos in the restaurant trying to calm our nerves, however, our imaginations ran wild, certain that at any moment they would burst through the doors. After an hour of anxiously waiting, we decided we were okay, so we left the restaurant and headed to our hostel. Thankfully, we never ran into them again.

Rules we broke: Not saying "No Money," hitchhiking in the rain

I really hope my two bad experiences do not deter you from considering hitchhiking in your travels. In both of these negative experiences, we broke our own rules by neglecting to say "No Money" beforehand or by being in a terrible hitchhiking spot and being desperate. I met lots of other travelers who have been hitchhiking for years without a single issue. I support intelligent hitchhiking because it places you in situations where you can meet incredibly interesting and unique people. For example, we met a cricket farmer, a music producer, and a coffee plantation owner. Not to mention, hitchhiking really helped me realize just how generous people can be. More often than not, drivers would stop somewhere and buy us coffees. A couple times they even offered us money!

There was one truck driver whom I think encapsulates just how generous some people can be. When we met him we were in Albania, trying to get to the border town of Kukes. He picked us up within five minutes of hitchhiking, and as luck would have it, he was going to the same town as we were. We exclaim "No Money!" as he laughs and says "of course not." He stopped at a convenience store, where he told us to get whatever we would like. Then he took us to a coffee shop where we drank coffee together. Next, he handed us 10 euros! We said no, we could not take his money, but he insisted. Unfortunately, something came up at his work, so he was unable to take us the rest of the way. Instead of abandoning us in the middle of the highway, he took us to a gas station and talked to every Albanian there until he found one that would take us the remainder of the way to Kukes. The pure kind-heartedness and generosity he demonstrated towards total strangers truly inspired me to be more generous in my own life.

Hitchhiking - Women's perspective

I am conscious that I am writing about hitchhiking from a male perspective, and as such, my experience is different from what a woman would encounter. Here I will include the opinions of 2 badass women hitchhikers I met during my journey. The first incredible hitchhiker I interviewed is a young French woman whose name is Justine. I was super impressed with Justine because, when I met her, she was 22, and at that time, I felt like she was already a super experienced hitchhiker.

1. How long have you been hitchhiking?

I have been hitchhiking for 3 years now. I started at home for about 7 km to go to the next village. I remember being really afraid. The first car that stopped was driven by an old man alone in a destroyed car. When he asked me, "where do you go?" I freaked out a bit. I thought the question was too personal... but it was just hitchhiking! Everyone asks you this question. I was a bit paranoid at my first ride, but when this old man brought me exactly in front of the house of my friend, I thought, "ok, those guys traveling by hitchhiking were right; people are normal just like us. Stop listening to the creepy stories in the media." A few months later, I took my first hitchhiking trip: around 1500 km throughout Croatia and Bosnia for a week. Currently, I have hitchhiked more than 30,000 km in several countries in Europe, and also in Turkey and

Morocco. I also hitchhike in my daily life in France.

2. Do you always hitchhike as a solo female traveler?

I always travel and hitchhike alone. This is the best way to be free, because you can do all that you want; you do not need to compromise your choices with someone else. Also, when you are alone, people are really more open to you, and you are more open to them. You are not in a bubble with someone else, but your eyes are constantly open to all the things coming to you.

Sometimes I can meet hitchhikers on my way, and we travel for a day or more together. I made a lot of good friends like that! I also converted a few of my friends to this way of traveling.

3. Do you have any sort of system or rules that you follow to stay safe while hitchhiking?

I always follow my instinct. People think only animals have a sixth sense, but we have it too; it is just that we do not use it and maintain it. The more I hitchhiked, the more I developed this instinct. And when my instincts tell me to not jump into the car, I listen. It does not happen a lot, but I am still really happy to have followed it the few times it has happened. And it is not about how the driver looks, it is about the atmosphere spread in his eyes, smile, expression, and way of talking. I have gotten into many cars that people would think, "they look like bad people, a terrorist, a rapist..," but my instinct told me there was no danger, and it was right. They were just nice men going to or from work. In the reverse, it already happened that I refuse to jump into the car of a man looking clean, because I could feel something wrong about it, and I am sure I made the right decision.

Another personal rule I use is to not let the driver ask me first where am I going. I ask it first, and then I take control of the situation. If I do not feel it, I can still say "sorry I am not going that way," even if it is not true. Also, it does not allow the driver (if he has bad intentions) to tell me "come with me I am going there too," even if he is not, because he could say that just to make me come with me to take advantage of me. But this never happened, it's just to take a little bit more of a precaution.

4. **Have you ever had situations with awkward/creepy guys? How do you go about fixing the situation to ensure you are safe?**

Two times I didn't listen my instinct. The first one was in Italy, close to Rome. It was 10 p.m. during summer. I was really tired and wanted to arrive really fast to my friend's house. Nobody was stopping at the gas station, except for one man. I could feel something weird about him, but I was too tired and impatient to wait more, so I went with him. Finally after 5 minutes driving, he started to scream at me, protecting his family, thinking I wanted to kill his kids (who were not in the car...). The second time was also during the night, I was with a hitchhiker I met in Turkey so I thought it was okay to go in the car with the two guys that stopped, even if I did not really feel it. Finally they were drunk and started to ask a lot of weird questions like, "what do you exactly have in your bag?"

In those two situations I just had to ask the driver to

leave me on the side of the road. I just say that I need to stop here, even if it's not true, then they let you out without problem. But when you ask that if you seem afraid and uncomfortable they could try to take advantage of the situation; just do not show your fear. For example, it can happen sometimes that a driver flirts with me, or ask me directly for sex. My reaction is usually always the same. I laugh a bit and say "I am a hitchhiker, not a prostitute, so it is not really appropriate to ask me that." Seeing me so comfortable answering that, the driver feels ashamed and embarrassed and he apologizes. Ten minutes later, we usually speak about his wife and children!

5. Do you have any additional advice for people who are interested in starting hitchhiking?

Absolutely do not listen to your fear, it will come at first because you are going right into the unknown, trying something completely new; your fear will grow a lot because of the people around you. Do not listen to them! They will tell you a lot of negative stuff, and usually that advice is from people that have never hitchhiked. When I started, a lot of people tried to discourage me, telling me I will be raped or kidnapped. But I have never felt in real danger while hitchhiking, and I am still alive with a lot of great memories, and I am even more happy than ever before. Every day hitchhiking is like a new surprise.

So it is normal to be a bit afraid, but use it to improve yourself. It is like riding a bicycle; at first you are afraid, but when you are comfortable with it, it becomes as easy as watching TV.

6. Can you tell me about one or two of your favorite hitchhiking experiences and what you learned from it?

Last year I was hitchhiking for 3 months in Europe. I arrived in Péniche, a city in Portugal, where I saw a van parked with a French registration. I did not like the city and did not know what to do. I do not know why, but I was feeling really connected to this van, and thought I should try to contact the owners. I knock on the window, but nobody answered. It did not mean I had to just give up. I entered a nearby shop where I asked for a paper and started to write a nice little letter saying something like:

"Hello, I am a French student hitchhiking alone in Europe and I do not like the city and do not know what to do. I saw your French van and thought I could try to contact you. I do not know who you are, if you are young, old, alone or not, woman or man, but anyway, let's meet!"

When I was going back to the van, I realize they were leaving! So I ran to it and made some signs for them to stop.

"Hello, I just wrote that for you, I don't know if it worth it now as you are leaving, but I thought to give it to you anyway."

They were a couple with their 15-year-old son and traveling for two weeks in Portugal. At the first time we talked, we all had a really good connection, and they offered me to join them on their trip to the next city. Instead of staying with them just one evening, I actually stayed almost a week. When I thought to leave, they decided to follow me to south of Portugal instead of going back to France as they had planned. After that, they had to go back to their life in France, and when I left them the mother cried, telling me I was the daughter she never had, because she only has two sons. A few months after that, in October, I came to visit them in their house in France for 5 days. They are my travel family now, and we talk a lot on the phone, calling and texting. I am also planning to visit them again soon!

Another nice story is when I hitchhiked in southeast Turkey, with a French hitchhiker I met there that was going until South Korea. We were in Harran, close to the Syrian border. This region is a mixture of different cultures with Arabic, and Kurdish, which is really interesting to observe. We were in the middle of nowhere, waiting for a car to come when we saw a little motorbike coming to us. It was being driven by an Iranian man accompanied by his son seated in the wagon that was attached to the moped. My friend jumped behind the father, and I joined the son in the little wagon. It was so funny! The father was driving really fast on long mountain roads. He was laughing and having fun like a child, happy to have us with him, while the kid was keeping his serious face. We came with them to a really tiny village with only farmers, where he had to give money to the man who sold him a sheep for Bayram ceremony. This is one of my favorite unique experiences from hitchhiking!

The next woman I interviewed is Stephanie, the person who helped me get started with hitchhiking in the beginning of my journey:

1. How long have you been hitchhiking?

Overall I have been hitchhiking for two years. It has been on and off. I take both public transport and I do hitchhiking.

2. Do you always hitchhike as a solo female traveler?

No, I do not always hitchhike by myself. I have done it a few times, but I prefer to hitchhike with other people. That way you get to share your experiences, and sometimes it can be a lot more fun. It is sometimes much harder to hitchhike with two people but it is usually more fun.

3. Do you have any sort of system or rules that you follow to stay safe while hitchhiking?

One rule would be if the guy looks dodgy, or whoever is picking me up looks dodgy, then I do not get in the car. That is the only rule I have stuck to. So far I have not really had to say no to getting picked up by anyone.

4. Have you ever had situations with awkward/creepy guys? How do you go about fixing the situation to ensure you are safe?

I think there is one time I can recall where a creepy guy picked me up. It was actually when I was hitchhiking by myself. I was in Bulgaria, and I was hitchhiking from a town called Plovdiv to the capital Sofia. A Turkish fellow picked me up, but he wanted something in return (sex). When he asked, I said, "No! Is there a problem? Do I need to get out of the car?" He said, "No, there is no problem, I will take you to Sofia." So I decided to stay in the car with him, and he took me all the way to Sofia. On the way he kept trying to talk Turkish to me because he did not know much English. He kept on saying I was beautiful and pointing at my eyes, stuff like that. A few times he tried to touch my leg, and I pushed him away. So that is probably as bad hitchhiking by myself has gotten. It is not too bad I guess!

5. Do you have any additional advice for people who are interested in starting hitchhiking?

Rule number 1 is always look over your shoulder and keep your wits about you when you are hitchhiking. Like I said before, if the person looks dodgy, do not get in the car. If you have doubts, do not get in the car. You can always say no to a person who stops for you. It is your decision whether you do or do not get in the car. So you have options. If someone stops and you do not like him, you can ask him to leave and you can get in the next car. Just keep your wits about you, I guess. Be strong. If you are a female hitchhiking by yourself, it is actually a lot easier to be picked up, but you do just need to be a little extra careful. If somebody stops and you do not like them or how they present themselves, just do not get in the car. You can always say no.

6. Can you tell me about one or two of your favorite hitchhiking experiences and what you learned from it?

My favorite hitchhiking experience was when I was with my friend. We were hitchhiking somewhere around Spain when this old fellow picked me and my friend up. He took us to our destination, but before he did, he showed us his village where he was born, then he showed us around. He then bought us lunch which ended up costing him 90 euro for all three of us to eat, which as you know is very expensive. Afterwards, he brought us back to his house so we could have a nap, and when we woke, we went to go get coffee. What I learned is that people can be very, very thoughtful and very kind. No matter how many bad people there are in the world, there are lots of good people too. It also was incredible to me how this old fellow took so much time out of his day just to ensure that we are cared for and protected. It is a fond memory that I will cherish for the rest of my life.

Section 2.3: Buses

If you are not comfortable with hitchhiking alone, buses will probably become your main mode of transport when moving between cities. For the most part, they should be relatively cheap. One thing to keep in mind is some countries have tourist buses as well as local buses. I typically prefer local buses because they are significantly cheaper, and you will meet a bunch of friendly locals on them. Local buses are usually more bare bones and rough around the edges. However, for very long bus rides, it might be worth it to pay the extra money for a tourist bus. The tourist buses will usually have some extra amenities like reclining seats, air-conditioning, snacks, Wi-Fi, and so forth. Tourist buses usually can be booked in advance online. For local buses, you usually just show up to the bus station and purchase the ticket there. Be sure to check bus times with your hostel or a local, because if the buses are very infrequent you do not want to end up bored at the bus station for hours. The decision on which to use is very situationally dependent and is totally up to you and your budget. Also, do not forget to continue checking flights with SkyScanner as well. In some countries, domestic travel is actually cheaper to fly rather than take a bus. For example, in Argentina the cheapest bus from Salta to Mendoza was $73 and 19 hours in duration. I went on SkyScanner and found a flight (with a checked bag) for only $45!

Section 2.4: Hostels

A hostel is basically shared accommodation with other budget-minded travelers. It is usually your most reliable method for finding a place to sleep, as nearly every city I visited had at least one hostel. The rooms can come in all shapes and sizes, ranging from 2-20+ beds, A/C vs. fan vs. nothing, in-bed power outlets (a big plus), bathroom ensuite, privacy curtain, and so forth. What usually attracts travelers the most is the price, which I found ranged between $3-20. Hostels in Asian countries were the cheapest. I could usually find a decent hostel for $3! South American countries also tended to have inexpensive hostels. Many times I could find a good hostel for around $6. European hostels were definitely the most expensive. I usually find myself paying between $10-15 (still significantly cheaper than a hotel). Cost aside, the best part about hostels is the social aspect inherently built into many of them. In hostels, you will find like-minded travelers from different parts of the world. Most hostels will have either a bar or lounge area which provides a spot to unwind after a long day of sightseeing. Here you can have a drink and meet interesting travelers. If at any point of my journey I wanted to meet people to travel together or to do day activities with, the hostel lounge area was hands-down the best place to be. There are a couple things you should keep in mind when selecting a hostel:

Read the reviews: But more importantly, ALWAYS read the 1-star reviews. Reading the 1-star reviews will clue you in on other traveler's bad experiences, and it can help you identify potentially serious problems. Sometimes people only read the first review or two, but this will not give you a good enough depiction of the hostel as a whole. Of course, do not let a single bad review taint a hostel if it has hundreds of stellar reviews, but if 5 or 10 people have all had a similarly terrible experience then you might want to reconsider. I have a story where I learned this lesson the hard way, and I will share it shortly.

Avoid bed bugs: If you have been lucky enough to never experience the torture of bed bugs, keep it that way! Those frustrating little stinkers are one thing I always try to avoid with a passion. They are a traveler's nightmare and can become your unwanted travel companion for months if they get into your luggage. If in the past four months a hostel had a negative review about bed bugs, I automatically found a different hostel. Most likely the hostel took the necessary steps to remove the bed bugs, but even the slightest chance of getting bed bugs is not worth it, so I would just avoid.

Understanding party hostels: Some hostels are specifically geared towards people looking solely to party, and these hostels will explicitly say if they are in their description. If you decide to go with a party hostel, just be warned that you will most likely be expected to come out and drink with people in the hostel, and that it will be loud late into the night. They can be tons of fun, but they are also super exhausting!

Use multiple hostel booking apps: There are so many different apps and websites out there with the sole purpose of facilitating booking that, if you tried to use all of them, you would quickly become overwhelmed and exhausted. I recommend using only two apps for a couple reasons. First, different apps will have different prices for the exact same hostel. I have seen price differences vary as much as two dollars a night. While on the surface this may not seem like a lot, as a budget traveler it feels substantial and goes a long way. Two dollars is a Pad Thai and an Avocado Shake in Thailand, for crying out loud! Second, all hostels are not listed in a single app, so if you rely on only one, you will not be seeing the whole picture. I switched to the multiple app method when I found myself in a pretty small village in rural Vietnam. I was trying to find a place to sleep for the night so I whipped out my phone and loaded Hostelworld, the app I had been using without fail for the previous six months. When I typed in the city in which I was located, it returned zero results. "Shit, that can't be right," I thought, so I re-typed the city name and hit enter again. Still zero results. Shit! I panicked for a minute as thoughts flooded my head of me needing to go door to door asking strangers politely if I could crash at their place, or having to find a nice bridge to sleep under, when I remembered I had previously downloaded another app, Booking.com. I quickly typed the city into Booking.com and voila! It returned one place to sleep. I was saved for the night.

Check the hostel location: Many times hostels are located in great locations, either right next to a train station or somewhere near the city center. However, other times a hostel will be located far away from attractions or in bad parts of town (you will generally find out about the type of area in the reviews). Although these hostels will usually be a little cheaper than competing hostels, when you factor in the extra cost of transportation, it just doesn't make sense.

Hostels in unsafe areas are also not worth it; do not put yourself in unnecessary risk just to save a buck.

While all the rules should be considered when selecting a hostel, I think 'Read the reviews' is most important. Here is a situation I encountered which exemplifies that. Please learn at my expense!

Getting money stolen in Thailand

It was my first time traveling internationally, and I had chosen somewhere truly exotic to explore: Thailand. When we arrived in Bangkok after an incredibly long and tiring journey, my buddy and I checked into our cheap hostel, where we had booked a private room. Before leaving for the day, we put our passports, credit cards, and $900 I had converted into the local currency into the safe in our room. I set the electronic combination lock and heard the cheerful 'Beep!', assuring me that our precious belongings were now safe. We left to explore the city and had a wonderful day. When we got back to our room, I immediately noticed that the door to our safe was slightly ajar. "That is weird, I could have sworn I locked it when we were leaving," I thought. Upon opening the safe, I saw that our passports, credit cards, and money were still there. THANK GOD. However, on further inspection, I realized that $300 was missing. A third of my money, the money that I was relying on to get me through my entire trip in this new and unfamiliar country, gone. I sat in shock for awhile, contemplating just what to do next. I realized it must have been someone who worked in the hostel and who had a master key to unlock the safe. A master key would be necessary in the case that a person cannot remember the code that they set. Furthermore, if it were a thief who had broken into the room and the safe, they would have surely taken everything. Therefore, it made more sense that a member of the hostel staff thought I would not notice if only some of my money disappeared. I immediately went to the front desk and explained what had happened, but of course, they said they had no way of unlocking the safe... bullshit.

The experience definitely sucked in the moment, but when I cooled down, I realized it could have been much, much worse. Thankfully they left our passports and credit cards alone, as it would have been a huge ordeal to get replaced, especially with it being the very first day of our trip. I am also thankful that they only took a portion of my money, so at least I had money for the rest of the vacation if I was more fiscally responsible. From the experience I learned two invaluable lessons that I have carried through for the rest of my travels:

Never carry that much money on you: In hindsight, I should have never been carrying that much cash to begin with; it was just plain dumb of me. But it was my first time traveling internationally, and I did not know a better way. Now, I have an amazing bank card that has 0% foreign transaction fees and will refund all ATM withdrawal fees every month. I talk more about the card in the "Essential Travel Items" section. With this card, I only take out three days worth of money at a time, which minimizes the amount which could potentially be stolen from me at any given moment.

Always read the 1-star reviews: As any angry person would do, after the incident, I wrote them a strongly worded negative review on TripAdvisor. While I was doing so, I read a few more 1-star reviews and realized that three other people had complained about the exact same thing! Although a quick glance at the place looked good with mostly 4- or 5-star reviews, the 1-star reviews provided the most damning evidence of why we really should have steered clear of that hostel.

After the incident, I have always been very thorough in reading the 1-star reviews, and since then I have not had a single other problem. It has helped me avoid places that recently had bedbugs, as well as potentially other theft opportunities. All of the other hostels have been amazing and fun, and are a staple method of accommodation in a budget travelers arsenal.

Section 2.5: Couchsurfing

Couchsurfing is hands down my favorite way to meet locals, experience their culture, see how they live, and save money at the same time. In case you are completely unfamiliar with Couchsurfing, it is a website and phone application where locals let travelers sleep on their spare couch or bed in their home at no cost to the traveler. After your stay, both the host and Couchsurfer get the opportunity to rate each other either positively or negatively based on the overall experience. Some people have compared Couchsurfing to Airbnb, but I think that is an unfair and gross oversimplification. Sure, both tools are review-based, and you are sleeping at someone else's place in a foreign country, but the similarities usually end there. This is because Airbnb is *transaction-oriented*, meaning you pay a prearranged price to stay at the owner's place. From most of my experiences with Airbnb, you would see the owner for the key drop-off and key return, but that was pretty much it. On the other hand, Couchsurfing is *experience-oriented*. The host does not receive any monetary gain from hosting travelers. Instead, the hosts are simply *proud* of their country; they want to share their culture with you and would love to hear about your experiences as well. I can safely say by using Couchsurfing, I had some incredibly unique experiences that I would have never had if I stayed exclusively in hotels, Airbnbs, or even hostels. Couchsurfing enabled me to explore abandoned buildings in Ukraine, get into locals-only underground clubs in Croatia, have large family style dinners in Romania, and so much more. The platform has done an incredible job developing a community of like-minded individuals who want to travel the world cheaply and share experiences. To take full advantage of Couchsurfing, a lifetime membership will cost $60. Being an official member will give you the ability to send as many messages to people as you want (as opposed to ten per month with an unverified account). This is an extremely useful feature if you travel for an extended amount of time because you will need to message lots of potential hosts. If you do not want to pay for this membership, it is not a requirement. Instead, Couchsurfing rewards users who host people. If you host someone in your house, you will get three months of free membership. Since I hosted more than five people before going on my journey, I had fifteen months of membership for free. In the next couple of sections, I will explain how you should act so you can get as much out of Couchsurfing as I did.

Couchsurfing - Is it safe?

The most common question I get about Couchsurfing when I explain it to someone is: "Sounds dangerous, is it safe?" When I originally told my family I would be sleeping on random stranger's couches throughout the world, they were super worried. While nothing is 100% safe, Couchsurfing is actually quite safe when compared to staying at other places. As I mentioned earlier, this can be attributed to the whole system being review-based. Every time I stay with a host, we both get the opportunity to write a review and rate each other either positively or negatively. As you can imagine, the more positive reviews a person has, the stronger the profile becomes, and the more reassured you can be the person is a good host. Throughout my 500 days of traveling and staying with countless hosts, I only had one weird experience. I have generalized all the various Couchsurfing profiles into 4 main types and explain what you should do when you encounter each one:

An incomplete profile: During my experiences as both a traveler and host, I would sometimes get messages from profiles that are incomplete. An incomplete profile looks like someone spent very little time creating it. These profiles usually have only one to two images, and very little (if any) description in the biography. I always ignore these profiles.

A profile with a negative review: If you see the person received a negative review, do a little digging and read the negative review. The nice thing is you can read the review from both perspectives (the Couchsurfer and the host), and from there you can make your own judgement towards whether or not you should stay with that host. I tend to simply avoid hosts with negative reviews because there are plenty of other people who are usually willing to host!

A new profile (0-2 reviews): This one is a little tricky because, on the one hand, I do not want to be put into a weird situation, but, on the other hand, I understand that some people are new to Couchsurfing, and getting the first couple reviews are always the hardest. In this scenario, I make sure the profile has a decent biography as well as multiple photos. If that all checks out, I will ask them for additional information like their Facebook or Instagram. Of course, use your best judgement, and ladies, please be extra careful about offers from men with zero reviews. It probably would be better just to avoid them.

A good profile: This profile has multiple photos, a filled-out biography, and 3+ all positive reviews. These are the profiles with which you want to interact. You can be pretty sure the host would be great based on the number of positive reviews the host has. For further validation, you may read all of the host's reviews. I almost always stay with these types of profiles. For ladies: there are many women hosts out there who only host women, so of course this is a safer option for you. If it is a guy host, make sure he has hosted women in the past, and that they have left him good reviews as well.

Once I find a host to stay with for the night, I almost always meet them in a public place first (coffee shop, train station, etc). If anything at all seems off or weird, just leave! You have no money invested, so your number one priority is ensuring you will be comfortable and safe. You may be nervous for your first Couchsurfing experience, but do not worry; just pick good profiles and your experience will be enjoyable and rewarding!

My one questionable Couchsurfing experience

While I have done Couchsurfing many times with fantastic experiences, there was one instance where the host made me feel uncomfortable. In the interest of privacy, let's say his name was Dave. When I met Dave at a coffee shop around 3 p.m., he seemed like a super friendly guy. After chatting with him for a little bit and deciding he seemed nice enough, I hopped in his car and he drove me to his house. His house was centrally located in the city and four levels high, with one room per level. On the ground floor was the kitchen/living room, the second floor was his room, the third floor was my room for the night, and the final floor had a rooftop. The one word I would use to describe his place: empty. For example, my room consisted simply of a mattress on the floor. There was no bed frame, no desk, no dresser, no art on the walls, nothing. Apparently Dave had moved back from London only a week before, so he did not have time to buy any new furniture to fill out the place. I drop off my things and Dave drives us around his city, taking me to various tourist sites and telling me lots of information about the local culture and traditions. The day turned into night, and we began bar-hopping around his favorite places in the city. About halfway through the night, he informed me that he was bi-sexual. Of course, I told him sexual orientation does not matter at all to me, but that I am straight. There were also a few instances of Dave being a little touchy (hands on shoulders/legs/etc) but I chalked that up to potential cultural differences. I have found that in many cultures, men touch each other much more frequently than my American male counterparts, so I was unsure if it was simply a cultural difference or he was being a little flirty. Not wanting to make any undue assumptions or come off as intolerant, I did not make any comment on it. After a fun night out, we decided to grab a few more beers from the local supermarket and finish off the evening on the rooftop of his house. Around midnight, I decided it was time for bed. As I was walking down the stairs, he grabbed me by the shoulders, pulled me close, and tried to kiss me. I had to physically push him off me, and I very sternly told him no and that I was going to bed. Luckily I had my own room, so I ran down the stairs, locked the door, laid in my bed, and popped in my earbuds to listen to music to calm down. As I was starting to drift to sleep, I was jolted awake by banging on the door—Dave was trying to get in! As I watched the door handle jiggle repeatedly, I gathered my strength and yelled through the door, "Go to bed, Dave! I am not opening this door, we can talk in the morning!" Thankfully he took my words seriously, and I heard his footsteps retreat downstairs. At this time, I considered leaving, but as I was on the third floor, I would have to leave the sanctity of my room and go down the stairs past Dave's room to leave. So yeah, not something I was willing to risk. I looked out the window and there was no ladder or discernable way of getting out that way either. I was trapped. Fortunately, the lock on the door was a thick deadbolt, so I felt pretty confident he would not be able to get in without breaking the entire door down. Eventually I was able to calm down enough to drift asleep, and thankfully, there were no other disturbances that night. In the morning, Dave was apologetic about what happened the night before, blaming the alcohol and saying he was drunk. I said it was okay, but that I would be moving to a hostel and not staying another night.

Throughout my years of Couchsurfing, that was my only questionable experience. I will admit, after this event occurred, I stayed away from Couchsurfing for about a month. One thing I want to stress is that if a Couchsurfing host makes you feel uncomfortable at any point during your stay, be sure to reflect that in a negative review on Couchsurfing! If you feel like a negative review is not enough, there is also an option where you can report the user to Couchsurfing. The Couchsurfing team will review your case, and depending on what happened, they will either reprimand the individual, deactivate the person's account, or even go to the police. This needs to be done because it helps maintain the integrity of the platform and prevents people like Dave from putting others in compromising and possibly unsafe situations.

One of many amazing Couchsurfing experiences

I hope that my one bad experience does not deter you from partaking in the magical experience of Couchsurfing. However, if it did, here is just one of many incredible experiences I had, which will hopefully help you to reconsider using the platform.

I was in Kathmandu, Nepal, and after hearing numerous times how amazing northeast India is, I decided to travel out there to see the region for myself. The journey was quite long and arduous—a 16-hour bus ride followed by 20 hours on a train. I was originally scheduled to arrive at 10:00 p.m., but as most trains in India go, it was terribly late and I arrived in Guwahati at 4 a.m. My Couchsurfing host had originally offered to pick me up from the train station, but as it was so late I assumed his plans would have changed and I would end up sleeping at the train station until morning when I would be able to contact him. To make the situation worse, it was pouring rain and my phone's SIM card was not working, so I had no way to contact him. As I stepped off the train mentally prepared for the worst, to my astonishment, I was immediately greeted by a friendly Indian man. My Couchsurfing host had waited for me—my savior! His name was Abhimanyu, a Mechanical Engineering Professor at the local university. He was quite the academic, and was very knowledge and talkative, ready to engage in intelligent conversations about a variety of different topics. When we arrived at his car, I was introduced to his lovely wife, Sagarika. She was the type of person who puts other people's needs in front of her own, an amazing cook, and was always making sure I was comfortable. Their home was situated outside of Guwahati in a more rural area and was an amazing spot to relax and soak in nature. When we arrived at their home, they showed me to my room where I immediately passed out, exhausted from the draining journey.

Their place had an almost magical aura surrounding it, and the next few days I spent with them felt like I was back at home. We had many deep conversations, explored the surrounding area, and did what I probably love more than anything else in the world: cooking and eating. Sagarika taught me how to prepare many dishes, such as Paranthas (kind of like potato and onion pancakes) and MoMos (chicken and onion dumplings which can be fried or baked). In return, I shared with them some of my favorite recipes as well: homemade pizza from scratch with tons of toppings, pork stir-fry, and probably the best thing in the world, chocolate and banana pancakes with peanut butter topping. Sagarika also took me to her older sister's house, where I met some of her family, ate a traditional Indian meal, and was honored with a Gamocha. The Gamocha is a traditional cloth typically given to respected guests, and this one was hand-woven by her mother.

Sadly, after three days, I left their home in order to explore the rest of northeast India. However, I was luckily able to return to Guwahati later on in my travels to see Abhimanyu and Sagarika for two more nights. This time, I was invited to Sagarika's younger sister's birthday party. Obviously I said, "Of course!" How could I pass up an opportunity to experience a traditional Indian birthday party? When we arrived, I was warmly introduced to her family, and I was able to see firsthand a house in which typical Indians live. Most importantly, I was served so much delicious food that I still have dreams about the meal!

This story is a great example of one of the best things about Couchsurfing: the opportunity to meet locals you instantly connect with that you probably never would have met otherwise. I am so grateful for my time spent in Guwahati with Abhimanyu and Sagarika, and feel honored to have known such warm and welcoming people. It was sad to leave for the second time, but I will forever cherish everything I learned and the unique experiences we shared with one another.

Couchsurfing - Women's perspective

Throughout my travels I have met lots of women that use Couchsurfing frequently, and who have agreed to answer some questions about Couchsurfing. The first woman I talked to is named Sherry, an incredible Couchsurfer with 50+ reviews, and she was actually my first ever Couchsurfing guest:

1. How long have you been using Couchsurfing?

I was on Couchsurfing from 2014, so more than 5 years

2. Do you most often use Couchsurfing as a solo female traveler?

Yes, as I always go traveling by myself.

3. Do you have any sort of system or rules that you follow to stay safe while Couchsurfing?

I only surf with local hosts by invitation - they want to meet me while they feel available for hosting. I will read through their self-introduction and reviews carefully, but most circumstances it is a type of instinct.

4. Have you ever had situations with awkward/creepy guys? How do you go about fixing the situation to ensure you are safe?

Yes, 99% of my experience are perfect and memorable. I was in Finland and had a poor experience; another guest and I even reported it to the police. We reported it to Couchsurfing first, but the user cancelled the account very soon thereafter. Then we called the police. I didn't really follow the case afterwards.

I don't really blame Couchsurfing, as a frequent traveler anything can happen at any time. Keep calm and make the right decision is a general rule for any circumstances.

5. Do you have any additional advice for people who are interested in starting Couchsurfing?

Yes, be kind to one another, be helpful as always. Personally, I do not use Couchsurfing as a way of saving traveling cost. Sometimes I take the local host to a restaurant for food and drinking, where I spend even more than I would have for a hostel or Airbnb. If you have no time to share with hosts and local community, i.e. in a tight schedule, I do not think it is a good idea to surf with hosts.

6. Can you tell me about one or two of your favorite Couchsurfing experiences and what you learned from it?

In 2014 I had a female host in Nice, who drove to the airport to pick me up and took me directly to a dinner party with many local friends. I stayed with her for a few days, then left Nice to explore other countries. After one month I was in Portugal and she happened to break up with her boyfriend. She asked me where I was, bought a ticket, and flew to Lisbon. We caught up again! Finding real connections among people is so fantastic!

The next woman I interviewed was Victoria, a Ukrainian living in Kiev. She is a good example of someone you can make a good connection with, as her and her son stayed with me in Washington DC, then I met them again when I traveled to Ukraine! Victoria is also an avid Couchsurfing user with over 30 reviews:

1. How long have you been using Couchsurfing?

I have been using Couchsurfing since 2012.

2. Do you most often use Couchsurfing as a solo female traveler?

Not a total solo female, but usually I would travel with my son. The first time my son Couchsurfed with me he was 3.

3. Do you have any sort of system or rules that you follow to stay safe while Couchsurfing?

Before I had some rules, when I was a beginner, I was trying to read feedbacks and everything like that. After some time I began to follow my intuition, and it worked pretty well, it worked all the time. I never had a bad situation where I felt unsafe, this might be because I usually traveled with my son.

When I stayed on my own, I never had any problems either.

4. Have you ever had situations with awkward/creepy guys? How do you go about fixing the situation to ensure you are safe?

I have never had any bad situations, either when I was traveling solo or with my son.

5. Do you have any additional advice for people who are interested in starting Couchsurfing?

Do not be afraid to open your heart. Do not be afraid to open your house as well. Just believe in people, people are good. If you go with an open heart with good and positive emotions, you are going to benefit from the other person. You will have a great time and a really nice experience because Couchsurfing is not just about staying somewhere for free, it is about sharing ideas, traditions, emotions, experiences; everything. Many people I stayed with became really good friends of mine.

6. Can you tell me about one or two of your favorite Couchsurfing experiences and what you learned from it?

As I have now been traveling up to 39 countries, I

cannot tell you that I have one or two best Couchsurfing experiences. Every single person is unique, and I cannot tell you that someone is better than the other. Of course, it is nicer when the person can spend more time with you because Couchsurfing is about spending time and sharing, which makes the experience more pleasant. I can also tell you that traveling with a kid is a very different experience than traveling alone. Usually people that accept those with kids are much more open to kids and kinder. Oftentimes we would be hosted by Couchsurfing families with kids, as well as we would host people with kids.

Couchsurfing - Being a good host

If possible, I highly recommend you host people on Couchsurfing before you try to use the platform as a Couchsurfer (guest). There are multiple reasons for doing this:

Meet people and get inspired: First and foremost, it allows you to meet interesting travelers. Oftentimes they have tons of travel stories, can give you tips on countries you are interested in visiting, and share with you their unique cultures. Before leaving on my 500-day trip, I would host people in my apartment. Constantly meeting people from other countries really elevated my excitement for my journey, and I received an incredible amount of travel advice.

Get some positive reviews: As I alluded to earlier, the entire system is based on reviews. If you have tons of positive reviews already, it will be easier to find hosts when you are traveling. If you have zero reviews it greatly hurts your chances of finding a person willing to host you because the host is not able to determine what kind of person you are.

Grow your network: Hosting allows you to grow your network of international friends, and this is extremely powerful. For example, I hosted that wonderful family from Ukraine for a few days when I was in Washington DC. Then when I was on my trip and happened to be in Ukraine, it was so simple to message the family directly to have a host. I started hosting travelers two months before I started my journey, but I regretted not starting earlier.

Get some cool gifts: Finally, you will start to acquire cool stuff from all over the world! Oftentimes Couchsurfers will bring little trinkets from their home country and give it as a token of appreciation. In my short time hosting, I received a bracelet from Peru, papyrus from Egypt, and mountain tea from Ukraine.

If you decide to host people in your home, here is a list of things to keep in mind so you can be the best host possible. All of these suggestions will come at essentially no cost to you, but make you seem like an amazing host in your Couchsurfer's eyes:

Provide your Wi-Fi password: We all rely on the Internet so much nowadays, it is common courtesy to provide Wi-Fi. Imagine being in a foreign country and not having data.

Leave out some snacks/drinks: Do not worry, you will not have to spend tons of money on this either. Essentially it boils down to the thought that counts. For example, when I hosted I would have a dedicated countertop where I put off-brand granola bars, chips, and tea. Then I would tell my Couchsurfers they were free to help themselves to the countertop.

Allow laundry: If you have a washer/dryer in your apartment, offer it to your Couchsurfers. Water is cheap and the Couchsurfer will be overjoyed with your generosity. As a traveler, getting laundry done at a laundromat is either expensive or a hassle; so, if you can offer this service to your guests, it is extremely appreciated.

Hang out with them: As I mentioned, Couchsurfing is an experience, not a transaction. The Couchsurfer would love to know more about your experiences and your culture as well. Do not stress too much about this; I am not saying you need to give all of your time to your Couchsurfer. When I hosted, I would let them know in advance I am busy with work during the days, but would probably be available at night. Then, if I was having a game night or something with my friends, I would invite my Couchsurfer along. There is one exception to the "hanging out with them" rule. If you happen to be super swamped, but you still want to help out a fellow Couchsurfer, simply let them know ahead of time that you are still able to host just unable to hangout. If the Couchsurfer is okay with it, then it is all good.

Tell them about your city: Tell your Couchsurfers about the best things to do in your respective city and your favorite restaurants. When my Couchsurfers arrived, I would sit him or her down and open up Google maps to get them oriented to the city with respect to my apartment and show them where to go. I also created a document I would simply print out which contained my favorite things to do and restaurants to eat at, just so my Couchsurfer would not need to memorize everything.

Couchsurfing - Being a good Couchsurfer

Be reasonable in your request: When requesting a host for accommodation, do not be greedy in the number of days you request. I had some people with the nerve to ask if I could host them for 10+ nights (they were always immediately rejected). For the initial request, it is safe to ask for two or three nights. After that, if you and the host get along well, the host can always invite you to stay extra nights. On numerous occasions I had a two-night request turn into five or six days just because we got along so well. However, if I had asked for five or six days right at the beginning, I am sure I would have been rejected.

Be a good communicator: Like with most social relationships, communication is key. Just try to keep in contact with your host to the best of your ability. If your train/bus/flight arrives late at night or early in the morning, give your host a heads up. Try to give your host your train/bus/flight information so if it is delayed, your host will know. Also, do not disappear on your host at night. Oftentimes the night is when your host will have the most time to hang out with you. Maybe the host would want to cook you dinner, and if you just disappear, you will miss out on an awesome opportunity.

Be considerate: Do not hog the shower or bathroom (especially if there is only one in the apartment).

Do not be messy: The host will allow you to use the kitchen, but do not leave dishes everywhere or not clean up after yourself. It is just bad behavior.

Bring a little gift: This does not need to be expensive or even necessarily from your home country. Functional gifts work as well: beer, toilet paper, hand soap. Personally, I enjoy a gift brought from where you are from. When I traveled, I wanted to bring gifts that would be relatively cheap, compact, and durable. So I bought 75 postcards displaying various USA landmarks (the Grand Canyon, the Statue of Liberty, etc), and after staying with each host, I would write a personal note on the back of a postcard and give it to my host. Use whatever you can think of, and be creative!

Be grateful: You have to realize you are getting a free place to stay! Not only that, but often times hosts are so insanely generous they will even cook you breakfast or dinner. Give them sincere and genuine thanks for their effort. One time when a woman stayed with me, all she did was leave a note that said, "Thanks so much for letting me stay, I really appreciate it." And you know what? That little extra effort to show gratitude was more than enough for me!

Couchsurfing - What you can save

Hopefully at this point you are excited to join the Couchsurfing community! However, if, for some reason, you need more motivation, I ran some numbers on how utilizing Couchsurfing could extend your trip. Please keep in mind though: while Couchsurfing is a fantastic tool to save money, please do not use it solely for this purpose. Please have the right attitude and use the platform as a way to meet locals and share experiences. If you do, both you and your Couchsurfing host will get so much more out of it. But, since saving money is what this book is about, look at how much you can save. In Amsterdam, the cheapest private room I could find was for $42 a night, and let's say you want to stay for 3 nights. If you utilize Couchsurfing instead you would save $126! Similarly, the cheapest private room I could find in Prague was for $23 a night. If you also want to stay three nights, you would save $69! Think of how much extra money can go towards beer and food now. Hopefully you can see that if you take the cost of accommodation out of your daily budget, you can reduce your overall spending significantly.

Section 2.6: Workaway

Workaway is an incredible website (workaway.info) that allows you to save a ton of money while traveling. The basic idea is you work no more than 20 hours a week doing some task, and then you are provided with a place to sleep and three meals a day. Think of it like a giant job board, where you can filter based on country and region, then read about the organization or person and about the type of work they would have you be doing. I have found that typically there are four broad categories of work you can do for a Workaway:

Hostel work: This can range from working the reception, cleaning the hostel, website development, or acting as a social organizer for events.

Farm work: There are many interesting jobs on Workaway that have you working on a farm. While the work is usually more physically demanding, it is great because many of the farms are striving to be self-sufficient. Types of work can be animal care, tending the fields, or constructing things.

Care work: Many Workaway jobs consist of a small family with either an elderly grandparent or a young child needing extra care. Some of the tasks will typically include caring for the person, cooking meals, and basic household chores.

English work: On Workaway you will find many opportunities where a family or a poor school would like assistance in learning English. Some typical tasks could be playing with the children, developing lesson plans, and of course, teaching English. Depending on the organization, some will prefer native English speakers over non-native English speakers, but it is usually not a hard requirement.

Like Couchsurfing, Workaway is also review-based. If a previous workawayer had an amazing or terrible experience, it would be reflected on the website where you would be able to read it. Depending on the type of work, the employer can ask for a minimum amount of time you are required to stay (in order to learn the job). On average the minimum amount of time you are asked to stay is a week, but of course nothing is stopping you from leaving early if the experience is just terrible. Remember, you are here to volunteer your time, and you are not under any sort of contract.

This is a fantastic way to spend very little money, really get to know some other awesome volunteers, do something meaningful, and rejuvenate yourself in order to continue your travels. To take full advantage of Workaway, they ask for a $42 a year membership fee ($54 for couples). I think this is a very fair price, because even if you do just one Workaway in a year, you will definitely save more than $42. During my 500 days of traveling, I participated in two Workaways for about a month each time. Both were absolutely incredible (and sometimes difficult) experiences, and I would not trade them for the world.

Thailand Workaway

For my first Workaway experience, I decided to spend a month teaching children English in a remote village of Northern Thailand. I had no prior experience teaching

63

children anything, and coming from a Computer Engineering background, I wanted to do something completely out of my comfort zone. I figured trying to teach Thai kids English would be extremely challenging yet rewarding, and boy was I right! Upon entering the remote village, my first stop was called "Baan Din," which means "clay house," and this is where six other volunteers and I slept, cooked food, and relaxed for the next four weeks. It was our home away from home. Although the name suggests it was made out of clay, it was actually made entirely out of concrete. They were extremely basic living conditions, but functional. There were working toilets, warm showers (sometimes), a decent kitchen, and beds that we were warned not to press up against the walls (to help prevent spiders and scorpions from getting in the beds, as apparently they can climb up walls then into the sheets). When I met the other volunteers, I learned that we would split up into teams of two, with each team being responsible for teaching a different age group. Team 1 would be teaching the youngest kids, Team 2 would teach the middle-aged kids, and Team 3 would teach the eldest. I was placed into Team 2, where the kids were usually between the ages of 9-12 and were considered the most difficult age to try to teach. I welcomed the challenge and said, "bring 'em on."

The village itself was home to extremely poor families, many of whom were immigrants who had fled from Myanmar. As I quickly learned, many of these kids did not have great lives compared to my childhood. They were forced awake by their parents at 5 a.m. to work in the tea or rice fields all day. Thankfully, school provided them some sort of release. When school was in session, they had an excuse from 10 a.m. to 3 p.m. to go hang out with their friends and learn something. After 3 p.m., it was back to work. Also, imagine the most poorly run school you have ever been to - I am willing to bet this school was in worse shape. The school lacked a superintendent, so the teachers literally had no one to hold them accountable. Teachers seemed to be in class less than 50% of the time, and when they did show up to class, their lack of care and effort was painfully apparent. As you may imagine, their bad behavior left a lasting impact on many of the students we were trying to teach. One unnerving thing was that some of the kids would walk around with weapons: knives, slingshots, etc. While I was told there had never been an incident, it was still a little scary when I saw it for the first time.

My initial assumption that teaching kids English would be difficult was right. Even just getting the kids to physically go into the classroom was a hard enough job. Everyday was essentially a game of hide-and-go-seek, as we would arrive to the classroom only to find it empty. It was then our duty to parade around the school until we located the missing kids. Some would be outside playing, some would be in a different classroom watching movies, and others would be hiding in the bathroom. Only after we corralled the students were we able to start class. But if you are thinking that our troubles ended when the kids were physically in the classroom, you would be mistaken. It was still incredibly arduous to keep them in their seats and interested in learning English. We would do everything in our power to keep them entertained by creating a multitude of fun and engaging games. Luckily, my partner in Team 2 had prior teaching experience and was a total rockstar in the classroom. Her name was Gemma, and she was passionate, fun, and able to command the attention in the room. Even with her abilities, there were definitely days where the kids beat us down mentally, and we would trudge back to Baan Din feeling dejected. Since we didn't know Thai, our nights consisted of lesson planning: creating flash cards with a picture on one side and the corresponding English word on the other side to use in class the next day.

We happened to be volunteering over Christmas, so we decided to throw a Christmas celebration at Baan Din for the kids. I must say, it was probably the most rewarding moment of the experience. We lavishly decorated Baan Din with tinsel and a Christmas tree. The other volunteers and I even took the time to develop a choreographed dance to "Rudolph the Red Nosed Reindeer." We made sure that each child received a gift bag containing a blanket, socks, and candy/cookies. On the day of the celebration, it was extremely rewarding to see how happy each kid was. There was food, music, singing, dancing, and a warm glow of peace and happiness that swept through the room. What more could you ask for in a Christmas celebration?

Reflecting back on it now, I think my time at this village in northern Thailand was one of the most challenging yet rewarding months of my life. Sure, some days I would be completely mentally and physically exhausted and think to myself: "I am not cut out for this, I am an Engineer." But then there would be other days—when the kids would learn a new word, and I could see the excitement and pride radiating from their eyes. Or when a student from my class would see me in the village and run up to me to give me a big hug while exclaiming, "Good morning Teacher Jer!" It was in those moments it all became worth it. I can safely say, with complete sincerity, that a week as a teacher for those kids in Thailand was more difficult than any week I ever had during my five years as an engineer in the United States.

Myanmar Workaway

To begin, I just want to say Myanmar felt like one of the most raw and authentic countries I visited on my journey. Compared to many other countries in Southeast Asia like Thailand or Vietnam, it is relatively undiscovered by tourists. As a result, the people are all genuinely excited to see and interact with a foreigner, which results in a lot of unique experiences. It was in this lovely country where I discovered the most inspirational place I have ever been in my life: Thabarwa.

Arriving to Thabarwa for the first time, I was definitely a little nervous and intimidated. The public bus dropped me off on a gravel road which I needed to walk for about half a mile before I would arrive at the reception building. As I trudged along, I noticed primitive living conditions. Tiny wooden shacks lined the roads with vendors trying to sell items like snacks or fruit. Stray dogs were rampant but very friendly. Trash was everywhere as there is no public trash removal service. As I continued to walk down the road, older people would simply stare while adorable children would run up with giant smiles, shouting, "Hello! Hello! Hello!" Once I reached the reception center, I was able to learn a little more about Thabarwa's history. Thabarwa is a massive meditation and refugee center located about two hours southeast of Yangon, the capital city of Myanmar. It was founded in 2008 by a monk named Sayadaw Ottamasura. The philosophy behind Thabarwa is simple: absolutely anyone is welcome. Whether you are sick, healthy, old, young, disabled, etc., the center will provide the basic necessities for life: food, water, shelter, and medical care. It is a place you can come to in order to grow spiritually, mentally, or physically stronger. When it started, the center was very small. As time went on, the center grew rapidly, and it now houses over 4000 people! Every single worker in Thabarwa does it strictly on a volunteer basis; no one receives compensation or a salary. Myanmar medical doctors, nurses, and dentists, as well as other citizens from around the country, come and volunteer their services at the center for weeks at a time. This whole system is based around the Buddhist belief that helping each other and doing good deeds will result in good karma in their own life.

On top of that, there are around 30-50 non-Myanmar volunteers at any given time. These people are travelers like you or me, looking for a more alternative vacation. The volunteers live in a four-story building named USA Hall, and each floor is designated for either men or women. The living conditions were by no means luxurious - what can you expect for a place run solely by volunteers and donations? The men's space was comprised of an open floor plan with three rows of eight sleeping spots. Each spot consisted of a wooden frame, a one-inch mattress, and a mosquito net. Some of the mattresses had bed bug infestations, so if a volunteer did not perform a thorough inspection of the mattress before selecting it, the volunteer would most likely acquire some unwanted itchy bites throughout the night—and believe me, bed bug bites are super itchy! I was initially one of those careless volunteers, but quickly learned from my mistake. The building had running water, but it was minimal. We were able to take cold showers, but we were asked to limit them to under a minute in order to conserve water for the others. Occasionally the water would simply run out, forcing us to take bucket showers in the center's public bath house.

Despite the lack of amenities I was accustomed to having from the developed world, I spent four weeks at Thabarwa, where each and every day was different, exciting, and inspirational. At Thabarwa, there are set activities happening at various times throughout the day, and volunteers can help out with as many or as few activities as they choose. I found there was no judgement towards volunteers who chose to take a break and not do any activities one day. While a very small number of volunteers took advantage of this system only for the free food and accommodation, a vast majority of the volunteers were truly passionate about the work they were doing.

The ability for people to find work they were passionate about was likely aided by the multitude of different activities available to volunteers. In the main building there was a large activities board, listing the numerous types of jobs you could do each day. Activity options included: collecting alms with the monks, cleaning the living area, helping the sick, teaching English, performing meditation, and cooking dinner. I participated in all the activities at least once, but I will only talk about the ones I enjoyed the most or found the most meaningful.

Collecting alms: The act of collecting alms dates back to the 14th century and is an essential activity for every Buddhist monk. Every morning, a group of monks plus volunteers would pile into a bus and drive to an area of Yangon to perform the collection. The act of collecting is actually very simple. There is a lead volunteer who runs ahead of the monks with a microphone alerting the citizens that monks are coming shortly. Then those who feel called will grab whatever they have to offer and stand on the roadside. A monk will bless the donation and the donation is handed to a volunteer who runs it to the truck for storage. What I found truly special about gathering alms with the monks was the sheer amount of people who showed up to donate. It did not matter if they were rich, poor, or somewhere in between; it seemed that everyone was eager to give something within their means. The poor would commonly donate rice, the middle class would give some sort of prepared vegetable dish, and the well-off would offer money or cooked chicken, pork, or fish. Seeing someone give a donation when I could tell the person did not have much to give was truly inspirational. It was also amazing to realize that the food collected during alms each morning was enough to support all of the volunteers and 4000+ people staying at Thabarwa for breakfast, lunch, and dinner!

Helping the sick: Many activities fall under the broad category of "Helping the sick", including assisting people who, for one reason or another, were unable to move. For the "Physiotherapy" activity, we would tend to various patients who recently had some sort of physical ailment, such as a stroke. We would massage whatever area was affected and help them perform numerous exercises with the end goal of muscle strengthening so they could move that body part on their own in the future. "Patient Care" consisted of volunteers assisting patients with cleaning and caring for physical wounds to prevent infection. A vast majority of the cases I treated were bed sores caused by patients being in the same position in their "bed" for long stretches of time. I feel the need to put bed in quotes because these "beds" were definitely not beds by American standards. Instead, they were usually just a wooden board. As a result, bed sores were rampant. Volunteers would go from patient to patient cleaning wounds, applying a sterilizer, and wrapping them in bandages. What was special about these activities was the interaction with the patients on a personal and intimate level. Although all of the patients had some sort of physical hardship, I was amazed to find their spirits remained high. Even with the obvious language barrier, the patients had no shortage of smiles or laughter, and they would constantly be cracking jokes. The overall energy of the environment was always positive. I think this positive environment may have been a result of their lifelong devotion to Buddhism, which taught them to accept all things, whether good or bad, with equanimity and resilience. This resiliency was reflected in the patients who were always a true joy to work with, and every day after Patient Care, I left feeling happy, fulfilled, and accomplished.

Leaving Thabarwa drummed up a wealth of emotions within me. Seeing people living in poverty is a heart-wrenching experience. I took solace in the fact that I was able to devote my time to help improve their lives in some meaningful way. After leaving, I missed the wonderful volunteers I got to know over the four weeks, each of whom I deeply respected. While some of these volunteers stayed for a few days, many stayed for months at a time. These volunteers helped me realize the importance and beauty of showing such paramount levels of compassion and caring to complete strangers. For this lesson, which I believe is best learned through experience, I am eternally grateful for my time spent at Thabarwa.

Section 2.7: Other cheap/free housing options

There are so many different websites out there providing free housing in exchange for some type of service that I could easily fill a book focusing just on that topic. For the sake of brevity, this section will focus on two websites in particular that have been used by my friends and whom really enjoyed the experience:

WWOOFing: WWOOF stands for World Wide Opportunities on Organic Farming. If working on an organic farm and learning about sustainable living sounds exciting, this could be a really interesting opportunity for you. WWOOFing is similar to Workaway, except it is specialized to organic farming. Like Workaway, WWOOFING provides a large "job board" showing opportunities in various countries. Each opportunity is reviewed by previous WWOOFers, so you can have an idea of previous people's experiences. WWOOFING jobs expect four to six hours of work a day in exchange for three meals a day and accommodation. There is no set amount of time required to work at a place. Instead WWOOFers figure out an acceptable amount of time with the host they choose. Sometimes you might just want to work a few days in one place, while other times you can opt to stay for multiple weeks. However, my biggest problem with WWOOFing is that, unlike Couchsurfing and Workaway, there is no international membership. Instead, you need to purchase annual memberships for each individual country. Each annual membership costs around $30. For example, if I want to

WWOOF in both Thailand and Peru, I need to purchase a ~$30 annual membership for Thailand's WWOOFing as well as a ~$30 annual membership for Peru's WWOOFing. This system did not work for my travel needs because I travel country to country. However, it is a very good platform if sustainable living and organic farming is what you are passionate about, because it offers more of those types of opportunities than other websites. While I personally did not utilize WWOOFing during my travels, I met lots of travelers who had participated in WWOOFing and absolutely loved the experience.

TrustedHousesitters: The TrustedHousesitters website is a fantastic option if you love animals. The website matches homeowners with someone who will housesit and take care of their pets while they are out of town. In exchange for taking care of their pets and plants they will let you stay in their house for free! The length of time the homeowner is gone can be as short as a couple days to as long as a couple months. The biggest downside I can think of is the price of the yearly subscription. They offer 3 options which range from the basic version at $149 to the premium version at $249 a year. The more expensive versions give you extra things like additional insurance and unlimited video calls with vets in case the pets get sick. While the initial price seems steep, I still highly recommend considering it, as I have friends who travel almost exclusively with TrustedHousesitters, and it allows them to save an incredible amount of money.

Section 2.8: Camping

Camping is another fantastic way to save money. However, camping is a very personal choice, and whether it is a good option depends on the type of traveler you are. There are many things you should consider when deciding whether you want to camp or not, for instance:

Is it allowed? Each country has different wild camping laws so, first and foremost, it is best to figure out if wild camping is legal in the countries you will visit. Wild camping laws refer to whether or not you are allowed to pitch a tent out in public. If wild camping is not legal in the country you are visiting, but you still want to do it, you still have an option: when you arrive in a place you wish to camp, go door to door and ask nicely if you can camp in the homeowner's yard. If you are friendly and explain yourself well, you will be surprised how often someone will say yes and even invite you inside for some food or a shower! I met a group of four French hitchhikers who were traveling the world with this technique. They basically hitchhiked as far as they could get in a day, then find a friendly person's yard to sleep in for the night.

Do you do it alone? I have met solo travelers who will pitch tents and sleep by themselves most nights. However, I do not have the courage to camp on my own. Everytime I camped, I did it with someone else. Not only do I think it is more fun to share the experience with someone else, but it also feels safer to me.

Is it necessary/worth it? Some countries have a

phenomenal tourist infrastructure, making it super easy to get by without a tent. For example, in Vietnam nearly every town has multiple guest houses where you can stay for $3-5 a night. In a country like this, camping does not make as much sense to me, and I never did it in those areas. However, in eastern Turkey, the tourist infrastructure was virtually non-existent and the cheapest option I could find for the night was a hotel for more than $40. Obviously I am not going to pay that much for a night and I elected to camp instead.

Do you want the extra weight? Camping requires certain supplies. At a minimum it requires a tent, a blanket, and a sleeping pad, which in total could add at least five pounds to your overall weight (if you carry it all yourself). This weight could also be substantially more if you want to cook food as well (pans, gas, spoons, etc). It is up to you to decide if the extra weight is worth it. When I camped, I only carried the minimum and would carry dry food, like nuts or bread, and eat my big meals in town.

Personally, I do not enjoy camping for more than three or four days in a row because I start missing a proper meal, an actual bed, and Wi-Fi. For that reason, during my travels I would do a mixture of camping, Couchsurfing, and hostels, depending on the country and situation. For example, I met a Spanish woman named Gemma, and we spent six weeks traveling through Georgia and Turkey. We decided to split the cost of a tent beforehand because we knew we wanted to do some multi-day hikes. We bought a basic tent for $20, and it really worked out well for us. Oftentimes we would find ourselves in a small city where there were no hostels or Couchsurfing hosts, and the single hotel in the town was like $50 a night. Because we had our tent, this was not a problem, as we could camp for free. Alternatively, if we could find a Couchsurfing host or cheap hostel, we would take that instead because neither of us enjoyed camping for too many days in a row.

Section 2.9: Restaurants

Eating foods from different cultures is one of my all-time favorite things to do while traveling. However, if you do it naively, you may find yourself spending a ton of money on restaurants. Never eat in touristy areas. Usually there is a significant price markup, and the food quality is not any better. I also try to stay away from using websites like TripAdvisor to find restaurants. Instead, when it is lunchtime or dinnertime, I recommend walking around non-touristy areas to find restaurants that are busy and filled with locals. It is usually safe to assume that if a lot of local people are eating there, then it must be pretty tasty. You will also find that these places are significantly cheaper than the touristy equivalent. For example, I used this method in Colombia and found a delicious lunch spot where I could get soup, rice, beans, salad, meat, and a drink for only $1.50. When I walked around the touristy spots, I could find the same meal, but it would be three times more expensive.

Section 2.10: Supermarket food

Another quick and easy way to save money while traveling is going to a supermarket to get food. Sometimes you will find yourself in a country where going out to eat is very expensive. Other times you might have had the local cuisine for the last ten meals, and you are a little tired of it. Personally, after eating heaps and heaps of fried local food I would think, "man, I just want to eat something a little healthier." Also, I have found while traveling that vegetables/fruits/meats/breads found in local markets are super fresh and delicious! For example, I was able to buy 2.2 pounds of delicious strawberries for only $1.25 in Chile. All of these are valid reasons to save a little money and go to the supermarket. While going to the supermarket every day for each meal would probably save you the most money overall, it is not something I would recommend doing. This is because I think one of the most important things to do while traveling is experiencing all of the different and delicious cuisines. Of course buy foods to your own taste, but here are a few quick things I cooked that are always super cheap, very tasty, and stupid easy to make:

Sandwiches: Probably the easiest, quickest, and healthiest: I would take fresh baked bread, local cheese, tomato, cucumber, and sometimes meat and put it all together in a sandwich. This is great if you are doing hikes or are in a place where you do not have access to a kitchen.

Pasta Primavera:

— Bag of frozen mixed vegetables (corn, peas, green beans,

etc.)

— Pasta Noodles

— Tomato Sauce

— Parmesan or mozzarella cheese (optional)

For this, all you do is fry the mixed vegetables for a few minutes then mix in the tomato sauce. Boil the pasta, mix in with the sauce, then sprinkle the cheese on top. Seriously, it is that easy.

Vegetable Stir Fry:

— Whatever vegetables you like, chopped

— Soy sauce

— Some meat (optional)

In a large frying pan, fry the vegetables and meat together with the soy sauce. Meat on average will take about ten minutes to cook. Use a lid to ensure more even cooking throughout. If a lot of the soy sauce burns away, you can also throw in a little water as well to provide steam to cook the food better.

Section 2.11: Washing clothes

Please be a clean budget traveler. For some reason, the occasional budget traveler thinks it is cool or something to be as gross as possible and not shower or wash their clothes. Please do not be that type of person. It is not very expensive to be clean, so just do it. When most of my clothes are dirty, my favorite option is to ask my Couchsurfing host if I can do laundry in their place, as often this is free and convenient. Alternatively, many hostels offer laundry services, though they can be a little expensive. Rather than pay for laundry services, I usually would hand wash my clothes. All you need is a packet of soap and a bucket (which you can usually borrow from a hostel). Just let your clothes soak in soapy water for about an hour, occasionally use your hands to squeeze the clothes, then rinse off the soap, and, finally, dry on a clothesline. I have found that synthetic clothes dry much faster than cotton clothing, so it may be better to pack as much synthetic clothing as possible.

Section 2.12: Free walking tours

There has been this trend in the past ten years of something called the "free walking tour." Basically it is a tour you can attend where there is no upfront cost; instead, at the end you pay whatever you think it was worth. There is no hard requirement to pay anything, and they will not single you out or anything if you do not pay. Most major cities have free walking tours, and they are an absolutely amazing way to see the big attractions of a city as well as get interesting information. I have also found, on average, that the guides who give free walking tours are more captivating and engaging than the paid tours I have taken. I think this is probably because if you pay up front, there is no real benefit to the tour guide to give an amazing tour or not. Instead, if you pay at the end, the guide will have more energy to try to earn bigger tips. So whenever you get to a new city, find out when the free walking tour is and attend. You will save tons of money and learn a thing or two as well.

Section 2.13: Putting it all together

If you incorporate all of the methods I previously discussed in your travels, you should quickly realize traveling does not have to cost an arm and a leg! You just need to find the right strategy to stay under your daily budget while still keeping you happy and experiencing everything you want to see. Like I mentioned, there are the extreme budget travelers out there who can get by on basically $1-2 a day. To do this they essentially never eat out, never sleep in hostels, and never pay for transportation. This works for them, but I do not think it would work for most travelers. If you utilize all the previous methods discussed, you can average spending $10-15 a day, which is so cheap! Some months I would do mostly only camping and hitchhiking, where my daily average was about $5. Other months I would be more lazy and prefer buses and hostels with my daily average at about $15. The point is: do what works best for you and your budget. Play around with all of the previous recommendations to see what you love doing. Each person is different and will lean more towards one strategy or the other. For inspiration, my strategy was typically as follows:

Accommodation: If I can find a hostel/homestay for less than $6, take it. If not, try to find a Couchsurfing host. If that is a failure, then camp or be forced to pay for a more expensive hostel (you will rarely get to this point).

Transportation: When moving around within a city,

always walk as much as I can. I use public transportation sparingly and only use a taxi as an absolute last resort (only if it is late at night). When moving between cities, I use public transportation if it is less than $5, if it is more expensive, then I hitchhike.

Food: Usually I will buy a simple breakfast from a grocery store like eggs and toast. I always try to eat out at least once a day. If meals are cheap (~$3), then I will eat out for both lunch and dinner. If meals are more expensive, I will buy lunch from the grocery store then eat out for dinner.

Fun: Since my budget was about $15 a day, any leftover money can be used for extra fun.

Section 2.14: Taking the leap

Hopefully by now you are convinced that travel does not have to be expensive. Even with only a small amount of money saved up, it should be enough for a lengthy and unforgettable journey. However, it may be difficult to have the courage for the initial push to actually start your trip. I know it was difficult for me. Making the decision can be hard, even when you know it is the right one for you. Even after I had enough money saved up for my trip, it took me several months to get the courage to quit my job and begin my travels. I had all these questions running through my head whenever I thought about it. Would I be able to find a good job again? What if I get homesick? How will I cope with everything? Deep down I knew that this trip was a necessity, but I still needed a little nudge.

For me, the nudge was buying my initial 1-way ticket to Ukraine about five months in advance. Purchasing the ticket essentially made the trip real, and forced me to come to terms with everything that was about to happen. This worked extremely well for me, because whenever I was struggling or having second thoughts I would think, "Well I already bought the ticket, so I cannot back out now." In addition to purchasing the ticket, I started telling some of my friends my intentions of a world trip. This is a fantastic nudge because research shows once you say something out loud you are more likely to do it. It worked wonders for me, and the more friends I told (even though I had nothing planned yet), the more real it became.

On the other hand, you may also experience some friends or family who do not want you to go. I come from a pretty traditional and conservative family, and when I told them my plans to quit my job and travel they were pretty shocked. Quitting a good job seemed like a crazy idea to them. Traveling to some of the countries I intended on visiting or sleeping on strangers couches seemed even more absurd. Back when I had my first job, I had booked a 2-week vacation to Colombia. My mom never liked the thought of me going to Colombia because she thought it would be terribly dangerous for me. It even got to the point that, the night before my departure, she literally called me and said, "Jereme, I really do not want you to go to Colombia. I will pay for your plane ticket not to go." I know it is a mother's job to worry, but she just had all of these preconceived notions about a country as a whole before even visiting it. She had the impression it would be super dangerous for me. I ended up going to Colombia anyway because I wanted to give the country a chance, and I absolutely loved it. The people were extremely friendly, welcoming, and hospitable. The point is, you may get some pushback from family members or friends. Try to understand from their point of view and explain to them why this is the best decision for you. Just keep in mind the experience will definitely be worth it.

Taking the leap will most likely be hard. You might have to quit a job you like. You will be away from friends and family for an extended period of time, and, as a result, you may miss birthday parties and holidays. But do not let this hinder you from going on this journey. The different cultures you will learn about, the fascinating people you meet, and the amazing experiences you have will be things you carry with you for the rest of your life. Take the leap; you will not regret it.

Section 3: Issues while traveling

"Traveling is a brutality. It forces you to trust strangers and to lose sight of all that familiar comforts of home and friends. You are constantly off balance. Nothing is yours except the essential things. -air, sleep, dreams, the sea, the sky. All things tending towards the eternal or what we imagine of it." – Cesare Pavese

Traveling is not always a walk in the park. For an inexperienced traveler, the following potential issues may seem daunting. But have no fear! We will discuss each one in depth, and by the end, you will be feeling confident and ready to easily tackle any of these obstacles head-on.

Section 3.1: Visas and e-visas

A visa basically allows you to enter a country for a specific number of days. If you stay in a country for longer than your visa allows, you could be fined, deported, or worse. Before I go into all the nitty gritty details of the visa, let me tell you about my most costly visa failure story. Hopefully something similar will never happen to you.

My total failure visa story

It was Christmas Day in 2014 when I awoke to a push notification on my phone telling me I was within the 24-hour travel window to finally be able to check in to my flight. A buddy and I had purchased tickets to go to Brazil for two weeks and had the whole trip planned. We were going to do a bit of hiking near some breathtaking waterfalls, and we had an Airbnb booked on Rio de Janeiro's most popular beach (Copacabana) to celebrate New Years Eve. I could barely contain my excitement as I filled out the web check-in form for my flight. As I hit submit, I was presented with a little pop-up banner which states: *You may need a visa to be admitted to the country.* As I read the message my heart skips a beat for a second, but I remain optimistic. "A visa?" I think to myself, "I have been to countries in Europe before, as well as a few in South America... I will be okay." I began frantically searching the Internet and found Brazil's visa requirements for Americans. As I read the list, my heart completely dropped. To obtain a Brazilian visa, I needed to physically submit a bunch of documents to a Brazilian embassy or consulate and then wait for them to mail me back my visa. The required documents included paychecks, an itinerary, the amount of money in my bank account, and much more. It quickly became clear to me that it would be absolutely impossible to fulfill all of the requirements and get a visa in the 24 hours before my flight was to depart. Going through this process in such a short amount of time would be unmanageable on a typical day, let alone trying to do it over the winter holidays. I learned later on that the Brazilian visa for Americans is known as a *reciprocity visa*, which basically means they make their visa hard to obtain on purpose because it is similarly difficult for Brazilians to get a visa for the United States. So while I could not be justifiably mad, and while I knew it was my own fault that I ended up in this situation to begin with, it was still very disappointing.

As the sad realization that I would not be in Brazil for New Year's Eve began to sink in, I picked up the phone to call my friend who was going with me, Ryan, to inform him of the terrible situation. "Ryan! I have terrible news. Apparently we need a visa to get into Brazil, and it takes a bit of time to get it. There is no way I can go," I exclaimed. As it turns out, he was in the exact same boat as me. He had also traveled in the past, but had never needed a visa before, so it was not on his radar either. Both of our plans were completely screwed. I called my airline and informed them of my unfortunate circumstance. They allowed me to cancel my flight as long as I paid the $300 cancellation fee, but thankfully I received the rest of the ticket cost as an airline credit I could use within the next year. Although it was Christmas Day, they refused to waive the cancellation fee. At the very least, I was able to recover a bit of my money. On top of that, we had to eat the costs of accommodations and flights we had made in Brazil because we were outside of the cancellation window. Overall, the experience was costly and disappointing, but it did teach me a very important lesson about researching and acquiring visas. To date, I have not had a repeat situation.

Getting a visa

The following section describes my techniques for getting visas for different countries as an American. If you are not from the United States, your visa process may be different, so please keep that in mind. If you are from the United States, many countries offer a visa on arrival, meaning you do not need to do anything ahead of time to get into the country. This is exactly how I found myself in the Brazil visa problem. I had probably been to ten countries before attempting to go to Brazil, and a visa was never needed. However, I learned after this lesson there are also a lot of countries which require a visa to be obtained before entering the country. Traditionally, to acquire a visa you would need to gather some documents as well as your passport and bring them to the embassy of the country you wish to visit. As you can imagine, this process can be a little time consuming and daunting. Luckily, as the world is trending to be more technologically advanced, e-visas have become a widely prevalent option for Americans. For every country I visited in my journey, a visa was either not needed at all, provided on arrival, or obtained online.

Do I need a visa?

Determining what kind of visa is needed, if any, is

actually very simple. The US State Department's website has general visa information for each country, telling you if it is required or not. In addition, it will tell you how many days the visa will be valid. A typical tourist visa length is 30 days, but sometimes it will be 15, 45, or 60+ days. Probably the most useful feature of the website is that it also contains up-to-date links which will take you to the official website of the country's e-visa application form. This is super helpful because, for many countries, I found that if you just do a simple google search, there will be lots of other websites offering the visa that are either straight fraudulent or will be a more expensive "speedy" service than if you were to go through the official website. Therefore, it is best to just go through the US State department website and save yourself a bit of money as well as a potential headache: https://travel.state.gov/content/travel/en/international-travel/International-Travel-Country-Information-Pages.html

Getting a visa on arrival

Countries have a few different variants for visa on arrival. The easiest variant (which is what I experienced in Thailand, for example) is you can just arrive in the country and get a 30-day tourist visa. Nothing else is needed. A slightly more difficult variant occurs in countries that have additional requirements, for example: a visa processing fee or a passport-sized photo of yourself. It is almost always mandatory for the visa processing fee to be paid in cash (no credit/debit cards), so be sure to have the money available before entering the country. Paying the visa processing fee in

USD or Euro is usually your safest bet, as sometimes the country will not even accept their own local currency. It is worth mentioning that usually the bills need to be in semi good condition. Do not try to pay for your visa with ripped or heavily damaged bills because the money will most likely be rejected. Also, do not expect to see an ATM before it is required to pay the fee. I was caught in this situation once before, and it was not the best experience. With regards to the passport-sized photo, there were two different sizes that are typically accepted: 5x5cm and 4x6cm, so be sure to have both. You can get a bunch of these printed at home, but if you want to save a little money you can get them done overseas (if your first country does not require them). For example, I had 10 of each of the two sizes printed in Thailand for just under $5, and I was able to use them for the rest of my journey.

Money problem with Laotian visa on arrival

When I landed at the Luang Prabang airport in Laos, I was filled with excitement for the next phase of my adventure. I had done my pre-arrival visa research and discovered that as an American I can get a 30-day visa on arrival, but I will need to pay a $35 fee as well as provide a passport photo. I already had a correctly sized passport photo with me, but I made a big mistake assuming I would be able to withdraw some of the local money out of an ATM before needing to pay the visa fee. At this time I was about five months into my trip, and due to my travel style, I had $0 of USD physically on me. Upon deboarding my plane, I found myself in an extremely tiny airport and immediately in the line where I needed to pay the visa fee. I anxiously scanned the room, but there were no ATMs in sight. When I got to the front of the line, I tried to explain my situation at the simplest level of English I could muster, but the immigration officer was not accepting any of it. He curtly told me if I could not pay the fee I would be deported from the country. My heart sank at the thought of not being able to explore Laos, and in the end, I was reduced to asking other passengers from the flight if they would be willing to loan me money in order to get my visa. After being rejected six times, I finally hit success with a super sweet Chilean woman named Maria. She empathized with my current predicament and agreed to help me out so I could actually get into Laos! She ended up being an awesome person, and we traveled together for a few weeks. While this story had a happy ending, please always make sure you have enough money to cover visa on arrival costs when you land. The added stress and worry of not getting into a country or needing to ask random strangers for money is not worth the risk. Later, I heard a similar but sadder story of an Australian man who was deported from Laos because he did not have enough money to cover the entrance visa fee, so just come prepared.

Getting an e-visa

Filling out an e-visa application form is also simple, provided you do a little legwork upfront before you start traveling. The forms are almost always straightforward, where you will enter basic information like your passport number, date of birth, expiration date, etc. The part where people usually make a mistake is when they are asked to upload a passport photo of themselves as well as a photo of their passport. Some e-visa application forms are finicky at this stage. Here are some tips I found to make the process more straightforward and simple:

Proper Format: When you take a photo of your passport or of yourself, have the background be white, and do not have any shadows in the photo. Make sure you have good lighting. For the photo of yourself, about 80% of the photo should be the length of your head, leaving 10% above and below. You can actually find some apps in the app store that will help make sure the proportions of your photo are good and will be accepted.

Proper Dimensions: For your passport photo, some visa application forms will want a 4x6 rectangle while others will want a 5x5 square. You can use an online photo editor you trust to do the cropping. I just google searched "online free passport photo editor" to find a great website that allowed me to do the photo editing.

Proper Extensions: Have all photos from above in both .pdf and .jpg format. Some websites will break if the extension is .jpeg, .bmp, or .JPG. You can use an online converter you trust to go from one format to the other, just google search "online photo converter."

Proper File Size: Many of the websites will have 1MB (or even less) upload limits. So you should take all of the files you created from above and shrink down the file size. Using the online photo editor from before can probably do this for you as well.

Once I had all of these files in various formats and sizes, I was able to use them successfully for every single e-visa application form I encountered in my travels without problem. I found it was beneficial to get this done before the start of my adventure because it was easiest to do the photo editing on a computer. I could then transfer the edited photos to my phone for when I needed to fill out e-visa application forms on the go. Here is a summary of every type of file you should have:

- passport_photo.jpg (shrunk to less than 1MB)
- passport_photo.pdf (shrunk to less than 1MB)
- passport_headshot_5x5.jpg (shrunk to less than 1MB)
- passport_headshot_5x5.pdf (shrunk to less than 1MB)
- passport_headshot_4x6.jpg (shrunk to less than 1MB)
- passport_headshot_4x6.pdf (shrunk to less than 1MB)

Filling out an Immigration Arrival Form

There is one other form you should be aware of, and it will be titled something along the lines of: Immigration Arrival Form. If you are moving between countries via plane, train, or bus, an attendant will usually hand you this form to fill out. Most of it is very straight forward and will ask for your name, passport info, countries you have been to recently, etc. The one part that might be unexpected is it will ask you for a "place of residence" for the country you are visiting as well as a phone number. Essentially, they want an address of a hotel or hostel where you will be staying. They never actually verify the address or phone number (as far as I have experienced), but they will question you if you leave it blank. To get around this, before going to a new country, I would just look up a random hostel's address and phone number in the first city I am visiting and screenshot the information so I am able to fill out the Immigration Arrival Form completely. This allows you to get through customs easily. I had a friend visit me in Nepal and we were going to go hiking in the Himalayas. When he landed in Kathmandu, he left the destination address blank on the immigration arrival form because he had a driver who was picking him up from the airport, and he did not actually know the name of the hostel where we were staying. When he tried to go through customs, he was stopped and questioned for over 20 minutes, and unfortunately there was no Wi-Fi, so he was unable to message me to ask for the location. Thankfully the immigration officers eventually let him through, but just save yourself from this potential problem and have an address ready when moving between countries.

Section 3.2: Moving between cities or countries

Oftentimes in my travels I would be relying on Wi-Fi because I did not want to purchase a local SIM card. As a result, if I was on the move, it was difficult to get access to the internet. From this experience, I learned there were a few things I had to do before traveling to a new city or country. I consider these tips lifesavers when offline, as they give me peace of mind in case I get lost or if an issue comes up.

When moving between cities

Set up accommodation: Have a hostel or Couchsurfing host set up for the first night prior to arriving in a new city. This gave me reassurance that I would at least know where I was going when I arrived in a brand-new place for the first time. I would typically only book a place for the first night, because I do not like to be overcommitted to a location.

Get offline maps: Download the offline maps for the new city. Google Maps offers a very nifty feature which gives you basic offline search functionality (for cafes and what not). Just open Google Maps and click on the top left, select Offline Maps, then download the offline map for the new city you are visiting.

Have directions to accommodation: Look up how to get from either the bus or train station to where you are staying the first night. Then screenshot the location or pin it on Google Maps. This way, when you arrive to the new city, you can use your downloaded offline maps and GPS to navigate to where you need to go.

When moving between countries

Everything from before: Use all the tips recommended for moving between cities.

Get visa: If the country requires an e-visa, have a copy of that e-visa easily locatable on your phone. I usually take a screenshot as well. You will use this photo at immigration. Sometimes a country will require a printout copy of the e-visa as well (it will say whether a printout copy is required on the e-visa).

Get travel information: Have your bus, train, or flight information downloaded to your phone in an easy to locate spot. I would also take a screenshot of these documents for quick access.

Download language package: Google Translate allows you to download most languages for offline translation. This is amazing when you need to communicate with someone in a language you do not understand. If you have the offline language downloaded, you can simply type whatever you want to say in English, it will be translated, and you can show it to the person you are communicating with to have them read. I cannot tell you how many times this functionality has saved me in one way or another.

Know currency exchange rate: Look up what the exchange rate is from USD to the local currency. Whenever I get to a new country, the first thing I need to do is take out a little money to survive the next couple of days. When I landed in Colombia for the first time I had totally forgotten to look up what the exchange rate was from USD to Colombian Pesos. While I was standing in front of the ATM it was giving me options to take out $20,000, $40,000, $80,000... and I had no idea how much any of it actually was. Do not play ATM roulette. Know ahead of time what the conversion rate is for the country you are about to explore.

Have proof of onward travel: If you are flying from one country to another, you may be asked for "proof of onward travel." Proof of onward travel is simply showing that you have purchased a ticket (bus/train/flight) which will take you out of the country before your visa expires. The intent of the rule is to ensure a traveler does not overstay the length of the visa; however, it can be extremely troubling for long-term budget travelers who do not know their next destination yet. Recently, countries have pushed the responsibility of checking for proof onto airlines. As a result, if you are checked, you will most likely be checked before you board your flight at the airport. If you are caught without proof of onward travel, it will most likely result in you needing to buy a last-minute ticket in order to prove you will leave the country. While it is rare to be asked for proof of onward travel (I was asked once in my journey), it can be an extremely stressful or costly situation if you do not have proof. As luck would have it, there is a little trick to get proof of onward travel at no cost to you, and the trick is called refundable flights.

Refundable flights

This trick revolves around airline companies allowing fully refundable tickets within 24 hours of the original purchase. There are a few online booking companies I know of that provide this service, but in this section I will use expedia.com as the example because it is what I personally use and am most familiar with. You can also do something similar if you go through a travel agent, but why would you pay money for something you could do for free? Anyway, the day before traveling to a new country, simply go to expedia.com and find a one-way ticket out of the country to a nearby country. Make sure the date of departure for this flight is within the range of your valid visa. Click on "Advanced options" and be sure to check the box that reads "Refundable flight;" this will ensure all flights you see will be fully refundable within 24 hours of ticket purchase.

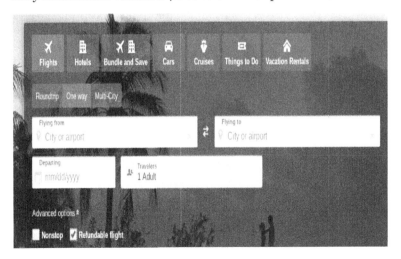

After clicking the "search" button, you will be presented with a list of flights that should all be refundable within 24-hours. Select the cheapest flight and perform a final sanity check verifying that it says "Free Cancel w/in 24 hrs."

Once this is verified, buy the ticket! When you get the ticket confirmation, download a copy as proof or screenshot it on your phone, cancel the ticket and get your refund. Oftentimes if you do the purchase then cancellation procedure fast enough (within a few hours of each other), your credit card will not be charged! Some people might think buying then cancelling a ticket is illegal, but do not worry, it is not. Travel agents have been using similar techniques since the first country started checking for proof of onward travel. To understand why you should always take this easy precautionary measure when taking a one-way flight to a new country, here is a story from before I knew about proof of onward travel and refundable flights, which resulted in me almost losing my mind due to stress.

My most stressful experience

I had just finished up an amazing time in Myanmar, and I was at the airport getting ready to start the next chapter of my adventure in India. Luckily, I had arrived at the airport two hours before my flight, because what unfolded next was probably the most stressful experience I had during my trip. I sauntered up to the check-in counter and presented my passport and Indian E-Visa to the woman at the check-in counter. After a few minutes, she asked for proof of onward travel. I explained to her that I would be heading to Nepal after India to hike the Himalayas, but that I did not have a train or bus ticket yet because Nepal was still two months away and booking a train or bus ticket in the country would be much easier. However, she did not care and refused to print my ticket until I had proof of onward travel. Thankfully the airport had free Wi-Fi (albeit very slow), so I thought it would be easy to book a bus ticket online—how wrong I was! On the first website I used, I found a suitable bus ticket for relatively cheap, entered the information of my credit card, and it was immediately rejected. "Hmmm, this is weird," I thought. "My credit card usually works. Let me try another." So I entered my second credit card, and it was also immediately rejected. "Shit! This site does not like my credit cards, surely a debit card will work," I decided. But no, my primary debit card was denied, as well as my backup debit card. At this point about 30 minutes had flown by (the Wi-FI was slow so I could not work fast), and I was starting to become anxious. "Okay, okay, this site must be bad, let me try another," I reasoned. For the next 40 minutes, I frantically tried two other sites with my two credit cards and two debit cards, and I continued getting rejected every single time. I even called my banks to try and figure out what was wrong. My banks told me they were not seeing any transactions and were therefore not blocking anything. Weird, right? As I found out later, the problem was that most Indian websites will only accept Indian credit/debit cards, while blocking foreign credit and debit card transactions because they do not want to pay the foreign transaction fee. They are able to identify what country a card is from by the first four digits and then only proceed with the transaction if it is an Indian card. This explains why my banks were never able to see any charges. Anyway, at this point my time before the flight took off was rapidly dwindling down, and I said, "Fuck it, I will just buy the cheapest flight out of India I can find and eat the cost." I used SkyScanner.net to find the cheapest flight out of India, entered my credit card information, and...DENIED. This time the transaction actually went through to my credit card company (I was using airasia.com and not an Indian website), but, unfortunately, they thought it was a fraudulent charge and blocked it. Now I officially felt beaten down. I could not think of anything else to do. None of my debit or credit cards seemed to work, and I felt like I was out of options. I was starting to think of all the extra money I was going to have to pay just to leave this dang country. If I did not get on this flight, I would have to pay a penalty from overstaying my Myanmar visa AND the exorbitant cost of a new last-minute flight to get out of Myanmar; it would be a very expensive mess. My head started to spin. It was at this moment that I noticed I had received an email from the airline with which I had just tried to buy the flight. The email stated they would hold my ticket for the next 12 hours, but if I did not pay in the next 12 hours then I would lose my reservation. Where I really lucked out is that every other part of the email looked like a regular ticket confirmation: it had a reservation number, all of the flight information, and the ticket purchase cost. The only difference was at the very bottom in big red letters it read: "NOT PAID." "I can work around this," I thought and used my phone to screenshot the parts of the email that looked like a valid ticket and avoided the big red "NOT PAID" part. When I was finished, I took a moment to ensure it looked semi-valid, and hurriedly walked up to the check-in counter.

Of course, this time, when I hand the woman at the check-in counter my passport and Indian E-Visa, she didn't even ask for my proof of onward travel and simply printed my boarding pass! I ran through security and sprinted to the gate, arriving as they were in the middle of boarding the plane. I was just starting to breathe easy as I handed the man at the gate my boarding pass, but then he asked for proof of my onward travel! I nervously show him my screenshotted "proof." He said something into his walkie-talkie, and let me through. Whew! I let out a big sigh of relief as I plopped down into my seat. Once again, I was just starting to relax when a flight attendant asked to see my proof of onward travel. This time, he looked at it more carefully, wrote down the confirmation number on my screenshot, and walked away. For the next 30 minutes, I was a barrel of nerves as my head flooded with the thought that at any moment they would discover my proof of onward travel was never paid for, and I would be escorted off of the plane. Time slowed to a crawl, and it felt like an eternity until finally the plane pulled off from the gate and headed towards the runway. I could finally breathe a big sigh of relief and thought, "I made it, I escaped!"

Since that ordeal, anytime I need to fly to a different country, I always ensure I have "proof of onward travel". I advise you to please do the same: book a refundable ticket, get the confirmation, then cancel it. This will give you peace of mind and you will not be put in the stressful situation about whether you can actually get into the country or not.

Section 3.3: Meeting travelers

For me, meeting other travelers is a super rewarding and inspirational experience. There are so many different ways in which you can meet fellow travelers nowadays; you will never be truly alone if you do not want to be.

Relaxing in the common room of your hostel

Most hostels will have some sort of common room where guests can hang out and relax. Simply relaxing in this area with a book or a laptop is a great way to meet other travelers. If you do this, you will easily find other solo travelers also looking for companionship. I cannot tell you how many times I did this and met interesting people who were traveling the same direction as me. Then we went on to travel together for weeks at a time.

More functionality on Couchsurfing

Previously, I discussed all of the ways you can utilize Couchsurfing to find a local host where you can spend the night for free. While this is the primary function of Couchsurfing, there are two other very important components as well: events and hangouts.

Events: Anyone on Couchsurfing is able to create an "event." Oftentimes these events take the form of a weekly meetup at a bar; however, these events can be pretty much anything, such as going to an art exhibit, a sporting event, or bar trivia. Attending a Couchsurfing event in a city you are visiting is a great way to quickly meet a bunch of different people from different countries.

Hangouts: Hangouts is a location-based feature of Couchsurfing where you say what you want to do today, and then, if people are nearby and interested, they are able to chat with you. Often times Hangouts will be in the form of: "I want to get a drink," "I want to grab coffee," "I want to explore the city," and so forth. When you find another Couchsurfer who is interested in doing the same thing, you set up a time and place to meet. Simple as that. I utilized this feature quite often when I was staying at a hostel but could not find anyone to hang out with in the common areas. This is a fantastic way to meet locals as well as other travelers. Frequently, I would use this feature to meet locals who wanted to show me their city for an afternoon and improve their English. Obviously, utilizing Hangouts will help extend your Couchsurfing network of friends as well. For example, I used Hangouts while in Bratislava and met a wonderful woman named Fanie who was living in Greece. Then a few months later when I was in Greece, I had a free place to stay for a few days.

Facebook groups

It took me a few months into my journey before realizing the usefulness and true power of Facebook groups. I discovered that for every country I visited, there was at least one active Facebook group for travelers. First and foremost, these groups are a treasure trove of information, ranging from visa issues to travel itineraries. Oftentimes I found the information in Facebook groups to be more up-to-date or relevant than what I would find from blog posts. On top of this, you can find other travelers who will also be visiting the country at roughly the same time as you. For example, when I was visiting Central Asia (Uzbekistan, Tajikistan, Kyrgyzstan), I had two issues. First, my passport pages were nearly full. I had enough space if each country did a simple stamp, but I did not have enough space if one country used a full-page visa sticker. I did a few Google searches online, but nothing was coming up with any very good answers. Second, there is a region called the "Pamir Highway," which takes you between Tajikistan and Kyrgyzstan. It is a pretty remote area which is easier if you have a private driver to get you between villages. However, a private driver is expensive, and it is best to split the cost between as many people as possible. So how do I know if I have enough space in my passport and find people before arriving in Tajikistan to ensure I do not have to pay for the cost of a private driver all on my own? The answer to both of my problems was quickly solved when I found and posted to the "Central Asia Travelers" Facebook group. A few days after posting in the Facebook group, I had an answer to my passport question as well as a few travelers who would be in Tajikistan at the same time as me who also wanted to cross the Pamir Highway. Pretty easy, right? So when you go to a new country, simply search Facebook for the right group. I found that, usually, the country name plus a keyword of "travelers" or "backpackers" work best to find the correct group. For example, if you are traveling to Peru, searching Facebook for either "Peru travelers" or "Peru backpackers" will most likely lead you to the right kind of groups.

Section 3.4: Accepting adversity

While a traveler's Instagram or Facebook account usually shows the most amazing parts of things that are going on in their lives, very rarely does it show any of the bad moments. While you are traveling across the world, more often than not, you will have wonderful experiences. However, occasionally things will not go as you anticipated, and you must be ready to accept that. Probably one of my favorite quotes that I try to live by is, "Prepare for the worst, but hope for the best." In essence, it means be optimistic for the trip and that everything will be okay, but have contingency plans in case shit hits the fan. The most common issue that occurs while traveling are when trains/busses/planes are missed, delayed, or cancelled. Other problems can come in the form of staying in super dirty hostels, being eaten alive by bedbugs, encountering really terrible weather, or getting deathly sick. Any of these issues could be detrimental if you were on a strict timeline, for example, if you only had a week off from work. However, since you are traveling for an extended period of time, it is important to remember a little problem will not be the end of the world. If you are extremely sick, simply stay wherever you are and get better. If a bus gets cancelled, remain calm and just find out when the next one is. If you really want to visit a beautiful lake but the weather is terrible, just wait out the storm. While it may be hard to get in a relaxed mindset in the face of adversity at the beginning of your travels, just remember you are not on a strict timeline, and things will gradually improve. The following story is one of my worst experiences I encountered while traveling:

A train ride from Hell

I was in India and needed to get from Rishikesh to Varanasi, which is about a 13-hour trip. First, I walked to the bus station only to find out that there are no direct buses between the two cities. "No worries," I thought to myself and walked to the train station to see if I could get there via train. As luck would have it, there was a night train departing in a few hours which would be making the long journey. Unfortunately, every single reserved seat was booked, but there were still seats available in unreserved second-class seating. I paused for a minute and contemplated the decision. I had heard some horror stories about sitting in second class seating before, where they load the train cars up so much that it forces people to literally be on top of each other or hanging out the doors and windows. However, it was a night train, so I reasoned that at least I would be able to escape the extreme heat of a hot Indian summer day and maybe even get a little sleep while it was dark. I went ahead and bought a ticket.

The train was originally set to leave Rishikesh at 11 p.m. and arrive to Varanasi at noon the following day. When I arrived at the station that evening, I looked at the schedule board and saw it was delayed an hour. "No big deal," I thought, "I will just rest a bit and then make my train." As it turned out, after every hour of waiting the train would get delayed another hour, and this cycle kept repeating for the next six hours. It was exhausting attempting to rest on the cold, hard floor of the train station for 45-minute increments, then waking up only to discover that the train was delayed for another hour. At 5 a.m., with my spirits low and still waiting on the platform, the train finally started to roll into the station. While the train was still lurching to a stop, people started pushing and jumping on the train in order to ensure they got a spot in the unreserved portion of the train. Fearing I would not find a spot after waiting all this time, I pushed and clawed my way through the crowd and jumped on board the train. After much struggle, I got to the middle of the train car only to discover there was not a single seat available. The only free area I could see was a small spot on the floor in the middle of the aisle. I quickly threw my bag down and sat on top of it, claiming my space, as tiny as it was. I wish I could say the train ride was okay once I was actually able to board, but unfortunately it continued to get worse and worse. Because of the six-hour delay, I was now riding in a cramped train with no air-conditioning during the hottest part of the day. We were packed like sardines in the train car and forced to sit shoulder to shoulder with one another. When my legs started to cramp, I at least had enough space to stand, but any other kind of movement was impossible. Because I was camped out in the aisle, whenever the train stopped at a station, food vendors would push their way past and inevitably spill a little bit of whatever they were carrying on me every single time. But the real cherry on top of this shit sundae was that I was sitting next to five misbehaving children. Throughout the journey, I found these children only seemed capable of crying, throwing sticky food around, and making a mess. At one point, one of the children literally shit on the floor. I wish I were joking or exaggerating, but there was poop on the ground for the rest of the train ride. The train ride was supposed to be 13 hours, but throughout the journey it accumulated an additional 4 hours of delay. So a trip that should have been 13 hours in total ended up being 23 hours (6 hours original delay + 13 hour ride + 4 extra hours of delay while on the train). Believe me, near the end I felt the closest to insanity I have ever been. I am not going to go into detail the kind of thoughts that were running through my head, but they were bad. When I finally reached Varanasi and got out of that train car, it felt as though a tremendous weight was lifted off me, and I was slowly able to regain my positivity and recover from this horrendous experience.

After the train ride from Hell, I swore to myself that I would never again ride in the unreserved second-class seating car in India. If all the reserved tickets were sold out for a particular day, I would wait for the next day to ensure I get a seat. The ability to be flexible while traveling helped prevent any future instances that could push me to the brink of my sanity again.

Section 3.5: Loneliness

Traveling for an extended period of time will definitely result in stretches of loneliness. While it is usually not hard to find people to meet and hangout with, sometimes it can be difficult to find other travelers. Traveling during non-touristy months can be a reason for this. For example, when I was traveling through Eastern Europe during the months of October and November, there would be times when I had the entire hostel to myself. I would be sitting in a desolate 12-bed dorm with only myself and the hostel owner to keep me company. Other times, you may just find yourself in non-touristy areas. For example, I spent a couple of weeks in the northeast of India, which is incredibly beautiful, but not on many traveler's radar as a place to visit. You might also want to do something no one else wishes to do, which presents you with two options: you can either not do the activity because you would have to do it alone or just go ahead and do it solo. The first couple of times I was faced with being completely alone, I will admit it was a little unnerving. I would get fidgety and was not sure what to do with myself or how to act. However, after giving it time, I soon learned how to be alone, and now I am able to find it quite enjoyable (although I still enjoy being with people more). To conquer loneliness issues, there are a few things I did which worked quite well for me:

Just relax: Try not to think about the fact that you are alone and simply relax. Seriously, your mind is your own worst enemy with this one. Before traveling, when I was back at home, I could sit in my room for a few hours just watching Netflix, and I would not give it a second thought. However, if I had a few hours to myself while I was in a hostel I would start to feel lonely. When I started to see my irrational way of thinking, I just framed the situation in my head differently. Look at it as another day in your life, and tonight you are choosing to relax. This did wonders for me, and allowed me to occasionally lay in the bed of my hostel watching movies all night without a care in the world.

Work on a skill: Working on something you want to improve can be a great way to combat loneliness. I know when I was working full-time, there were lots of things I would want to do, but after work I would just be too tired to dedicate time to do them. Utilizing free time while you are traveling can be a great thing. What I found myself doing the most often whenever I had downtime was learning Spanish on DuoLingo, reading interesting books that other travelers had recommended to me, or trying to write this book! Just choose something you want to improve and go for it. One thing travelers love to do is learn an instrument, so if you are musically motivated, you can learn to play guitar or drums and people will love you for it! Often times hostels have a guitar laying around if you need extra motivation to practice your skills.

Planning: While basic planning is the least sexy of the options, in my opinion, it is a necessary component to traveling the world. At the very least you should be sure to apply for visas for countries you are going to in the near term. In addition, I typically plan my trip (city-wise) about 2-3 days in advance. This gives me enough time to find either a hostel or someone on Couchsurfing who is willing to host me. Also, I use this time to get a general sense of activities I wish to do in the next city.

Get lost in thought: Getting lost in thought is a great way to combat loneliness and is easy to do. Just pick some topic or idea and think it all the way through. Think about it from all possible angles and different perspectives. You might be surprised by what you find out about yourself. This was my favorite thing to do whenever I found myself solo hiking somewhere. It is not an activity I can do just sitting in a chair because I get too restless, but if my legs are moving I found it to be absolutely perfect. There is literally no limit to what you can think about, throughout my travels I have probably exhausted every topic I could imagine. Some things I have thought about that I found very interesting were: whether I could ever adopt, past relationships, short-term life goals, long-term life goals, and my definitions of love, religion, our political system. The list goes on and on.

Section 3.6: Missing events back home

Some of the hardest moments for me during my time abroad was definitely missing family or friend events back home. Even though traveling offers you this enormous amount of new, fun, and exciting experiences, you will still succumb to a feeling of sadness when you realize you missed your little niece's birthday, a good friend's wedding, or a big family reunion. Thankfully, with the gift of modern technology, there are numerous methods with which you can stay in touch with your loved ones, even though you are thousands of miles apart.

Video chat for the big events: Thankfully, there are so many video chat technologies out there (Zoom, WhatsApp, Messenger, etc) that you never have to completely miss an event if you do not want to do so. That is why I recommend you video chat for some of the big events. Something to consider, though, is although the technology is a great step in the right direction, it is not a complete substitute for you actually being there. It is easier to forget about a person if they are not literally sitting in the room, or the phone may fall and you find yourself staring at the ceiling for a few minutes. Another thing to remember is where you are in the world. Depending on where you are, you might find yourself needing to stay up until 3 or 4 in the morning in order to celebrate a holiday with your family.

Setup recurrent times to talk: This one was huge for me, and it definitely helped keep some of my sanity throughout my travels. While messaging apps are great for quick little updates, there is still something special about a voice or video call. For this reason, I would try to set up monthly calls with my friends, and weekly calls with my parents. Everybody has very busy lives, and I found that trying to schedule calls too frequently can be difficult, especially with different time zones. For example, when I was in India, I was 12 hours apart from my family, so I would usually only have the opportunity to talk when it was in the early morning for me and at night for them. However, if you can get a time where everyone's schedules work out, these little chats are simply amazing. It is super refreshing to hear about things going on in your friends and family lives, so I highly recommend making the effort.

Send little gifts: You will inevitably miss some social events while you are traveling. Missing these events will usually be okay, and your friends and family will probably understand if you do not get them gifts while you are trying to budget travel. However, this doesn't mean you should completely neglect the ones you love. For this reason, I would try to send little gifts sporadically throughout my travels. The easiest, simplest, and most cost-effective option are definitely postcards. You can buy them anywhere in the world, they capture the place you are currently at, and you can write a short heartfelt message on them. One thing to remember is that you cannot expect punctuality with postcards. I have had postcards take 6, 8, or even 10+ weeks until they arrive at their destination. I would typically send postcards at random times throughout my travels, as it shows the ones you love that you are thinking of them, even when it is not a particular holiday or event.

Section 3.7: Dealing with the homeless/poor

If you are coming from a traditionally wealthy country in particular, you will probably feel some level of shock for the first time when you visit certain countries due to the vast amount of homeless people living in extreme poverty. I know when I visited India for the first time, it was daunting riding the bus, glancing out the window and seeing hundreds of homeless people scattered along the highway. Their nicer "houses" were constructed out of simple wooden beams, while the ultra-poor had habitats made of cardboard or even oftentimes nothing. Probably the hardest part to see were the children. Typically they would look like they had not showered for weeks and were dressed in tattered clothing. They would always come up and ask for a picture, then immediately ask for money. Also, I found out that oftentimes families would "use" children in order to have higher chances of extracting money from tourists. This can come in the form of purposely making their kids look sick, then telling them not to move when tourists walk by them. In other cases, the parents will take the kids out of school and have the children play by the road or use them to sell various trinkets to try to get money. Since I believe education is the key to ultimately overcoming poverty, this is clearly something I cannot support. In extreme cases, I heard of parents literally hurting their kids to a point where they have a physical disability. Absolutely terrible! What am I to do? The problem is if I were to give even 25 cents to every person who asked for money while I was traveling, I would most likely give out more than $15 every day!

While giving money was something clearly I could not afford as a budget traveler, I came up with a different strategy where I could feel like I was truly helping those whom legitimately wanted help, while weeding out the people who were simply trying to siphon money out of travelers. While I can acknowledge it is not a perfect solution, it worked for me. If I knew I would be traveling to an ultra-touristy location where inevitably lots of beggars would be, I would buy some type of food that is very cheap and comes in a large quantity. For example, I could buy about 20 mini bananas for about 50 cents, or a very large bag of raisins for about 1 dollar. Then whenever a child asked for money, I would offer up a piece of food instead. If the child was simply "working" to extract money from travelers, the food would usually be rudely turned down. Instead, if the child really was in a bad situation and needed something to eat, the food would be gladly received. To me, it felt more rewarding giving food because, more times than not, the child's eyes would grow wide with a big smile on his or her face as the food that I had offered was taken.

Offering food in Angkor Wat

Angkor Wat is the most touristy place in Cambodia, so when I went I was not excited at the thought of being constantly asked for money by beggars. Before heading to the temples, I used my strategy and bought about 20 mini bananas to use as donations. Shortly thereafter, I was sitting outside a temple enjoying my breakfast when a young girl of about 10 approached me and started asking for money. I politely declined, but added that she was more than welcome to sit with me and enjoy some of my breakfast. She happily obliged and settled in beside me. While I have no idea how her name was actually spelt, it sounded like "Two." Two was a very smart girl whose English was surprisingly good for it not being her first language, as she was able to make jokes and even picked up on my sarcastic sense of humor. She informed me that she was not missing school (thankfully), and that it didn't start until 11 a.m. Her favorite subject is Math, she loves playing basketball/football, and when she grows up she wants to become a nurse. After about 20 minutes of chatting, she was pulled away by her mother who wanted her "working" to get more money, and I felt sad to see her leave. While this may sound like a very simple and brief interaction, to me it was an amazing experience. Seeing beyond a typically aggressive street beggar and seeing more depth into who they actually are as individuals was really quite refreshing. This would not have occurred if I had simply given her money and not offered a little food to eat.

Section 3.8: Travel fatigue

My usual travel pattern would be visiting a new city for two or three days to see and experience as much as possible, then move to the next city. While this pattern is great to see as much as possible, it is also draining. Moving from place to place is physically draining with needing to pack and repack your bag and get to the bus or train station so often. On top of that, you meet so many new people every couple days in hostels, and that it is mentally draining as well. Your friends and family back home might not understand it and ask: "How can you be exhausted if you are just *traveling*." Well let me tell you that travel fatigue is definitely a thing, and it will inevitably happen to you if you travel for a long enough period of time. I like to tell my friends that "I am taking a vacation from my vacation" when I hit this point of fatigue.

Take a day off: One thing I needed to learn when traveling for an extended period of time, and not just a two-week vacation, is that time is not such a relevant issue. When I was working and only had a two-week vacation, I would find myself cramming as much as possible into those two weeks in order to maximize my time. Early into my journey, I found myself doing the exact same thing. However, I quickly realized that method of traveling is simply not sustainable for long periods of time; I needed to slow down. To do that, I started taking a relaxation day periodically. For me personally, I found taking a day off about every 14 days is a fantastic way to stay fresh. On my days off, I would often work out at a gymnasium, eat lots of yummy food, learn some Spanish, and read/write. On your day off, just do whatever makes YOU happy. It could be learning guitar, trying to paint, or playing some soccer with local kids. Just relax and recover!

Take a couple weeks off: After a certain amount of time, simply taking a day off here or there will not be sufficient, unfortunately. Your body will ache for something that feels more like home, more like a community. This first hit me about four and a half months into my travels, after a whirlwind tour of Eastern Europe. I was tired of meeting people for a couple of days only to part ways shortly after. I was tired of moving between places all the time. When you start to feel this way, I found the best solution is to stay in the same place for a couple weeks and build a stronger relationship with the people and area. For me personally, I would find myself needing to take a couple weeks "off" about every four months. I found that things like Workaway or WWOOFing are absolutely the best for when you get serious travel fatigue. For my first Workaway experience, I spent a month in a remote village of Northern Thailand teaching little kids English with six other amazing volunteers. Not only was this Workaway experience rewarding, but staying in one place for a month and really getting to know six amazing individuals totally rejuvenated me for the next part of my journey.

Section 3.9: Staying connected

Let's face it, most of us are all pretty heavily tied to our phones, so being able to stay connected to the outside world is crucial, even while traveling. Luckily for us, we live in a world where free Wi-Fi is prevalent in most countries. In many countries I visited, I had no problems whatsoever finding and connecting to an open Wi-Fi. I have two suggestions which will allow you to be connected in nearly any situation you find yourself.

WiFi Map

There is a nifty little app called WiFi Map I have used successfully time and time again in medium to large cities. This app is great when you find yourself in a city where all of the Wi-Fi networks are password protected. In this situation, open the app, and it will use your geo-location to find nearby Wi-Fi networks for which it knows the password. Then you can connect to that network with the known password. How this works under the hood is that the database of known passwords is *crowd sourced*. That means the more people who contribute, the better and more effective the app will be. Here is an example: say you are at a pizza restaurant named Awesome Pizzeria. You find out the password for Awesome Pizzeria's Wi-Fi network is 12345678. If you load this information into the WiFi Map app, then other people using the app will now be able to discover the password for Awesome Pizzeria's Wi-Fi network and will be able to login to it. In this case, sharing really is caring, and the more people who contribute information the better the app becomes.

Foreign SIM cards

Unlike in the USA where a phone plan is expensive, in other parts of the world data is cheap cheap cheap! For example, in Ukraine the SIM card I purchased provided 10GB of data and cost me a whopping $3. At those prices, it would be crazy not to buy a foreign SIM card. Most places will do the SIM card replacement for you as well, so you will have a working foreign SIM card before you leave the store. If I stayed in a country for more than a couple weeks, I would typically buy a foreign SIM card. It really does come in handy for long bus/train rides. Also if I was in a country where I knew I would want to do a lot a hitchhiking, I would almost always buy a local SIM card. I would do this for two reasons. First, if for some reason hitchhiking gets me stranded in the middle of nowhere, at least I will have data to message people or get help. Second, with data I can use my Google Translate's voice-to-translate feature, which is an absolutely fantastic way to converse with the person who is giving you a ride. If I was only staying in a country for a week or less, then buying a local SIM card was probably not super critical. The only prerequisite to using foreign SIM cards is that your phone must be unlocked.

Unlocked phone: This problem is most likely specific to Americans, as in many other countries phones come unlocked by default. However, in the United States, things are usually a little different. You know how when you buy a new phone, the phone comes with a big discount if you buy a service plan (usually a two-year commitment)? Well that is because the service providers make most of their money through the service plan, which allows them to heavily discount the initial cost of the phone. To prevent you from breaking contract and switching to a different provider, they insert a "phone lock." This phone lock becomes a problem when you are traveling overseas and wish to buy a foreign SIM card. To unlock your phone, it is typically as simple as calling your service provider, telling them you are traveling overseas, and they will unlock it for you. Sometimes they will tell you to download an app that will handle the unlocking process. Either way, make sure you do this before traveling overseas. I was naive when I started my travels and assumed my phone was already unlocked (it was not). It was a big headache getting it resolved overseas, so it would probably be best to make sure it gets done beforehand.

One issue that might come up when using a foreign SIM card is that you will most likely lose your old phone number (because oftentimes the phone number is tied to the SIM card). This can cause a problem if friends from your home country try to text or call you on your old number. For this reason, I recommend that you *port* your original number to an Internet based messaging service (like Google Voice) before starting to travel abroad. Porting your number basically means moving your telephone number from one company to another. If you ever switched phone companies in the USA and were able to keep your old phone number, it means you ported your phone number from your old service provider to your new one.

What is an Internet-based messaging service?

At its core, an Internet-based messaging service

provides all the functionality of texting, but does it over the Internet instead of the regular texting protocol. What this means is that as long as I have data turned on on my phone, I will be able to receive my text messages. The Internet based messaging service of my choice is Google Voice. Using this application, I can move around from country to country, plugging in any SIM card that I liked. As long as the SIM card is a part of a data plan, I will continue to receive messages/calls on my old number as if I had never even swapped SIM cards! This is a lifesaver as you travel around because you will never need to remember any new phone numbers, and your friends from back home can still text you as if nothing has ever changed.

Section 3.10: Travel insurance

Traveling abroad is not always sunshine and butterflies, bad things can happen at any moment. I am not saying this to deter you from wanting to travel, but it is something you should consider. Things getting stolen, flight cancelations, and injury are all possible during a long journey. As such, if you are traveling for an extended time, I would highly recommend getting travel insurance. Having travel insurance has given me peace of mind that, if I were in some sort of accident, I would be covered. I have heard enough travel nightmares where a traveler gets in a pretty serious accident, needs to undergo multiple surgeries, and racks up a gigantic bill that is near impossible to pay off. If you already have health insurance, check whether your policy includes coverage while overseas. I have found that most insurance policies will not cover international bills. Ergo, why I recommend travel insurance. In my experience, most travel insurance policies will offer medical emergency evacuation coverage and cover international hospital bills.

Travel insurance can help with smaller problems as well. If a flight gets cancelled or delayed, certain policies will refund you for the cost of the flight. If your luggage or backpack gets stolen, you may be able to be reimbursed for the contents of the stolen items. Some policies will even replace your phone if it gets stolen or breaks. This is an especially nice feature, in my opinion, as I feel phones are often targeted the most for theft.

For my 500 days abroad, I was covered by World Nomads Insurance for less than $3 a day. However, there are lots of travel insurance companies out there, so you should hunt around for the cheapest and best option for your budget. I chose World Nomads for its low cost and based on recommendations from friends who had used it. That said, I have been extremely lucky and never actually had to put my travel insurance to use. There were two close calls where my phone was almost stolen, but thankfully the thief did not succeed (more on that later). However, I was traveling with a friend I met named Garrett for about ten days, and during that time he was not so fortunate. We were in Armenia trying to hitchhike from one town to another, but we were feeling lazy and did not want to walk very far. Instead of starting in a great hitchhiking spot, we found ourselves trying to hitchhike near the center of town. After about ten minutes of failure, a construction worker came up and started talking to us in Armenian. Because we did not speak Armenian, and he didn't speak English, he was being very emphatic with his hand gestures. Essentially, he was trying to tell us we were not in a good spot, and in the process he knocked Garrett's phone right out of his hand. Thud! The phone landed face down on the pavement. When Garrett picked up the phone, the screen was completely busted. Luckily, Garrett had travel insurance. He called his travel insurance company, explained his story, and was informed he would be covered! All he needed to do was take the phone to a repair shop and get a quote on how expensive it would be to fix the screen. If the repair was more expensive than the cost of the phone, then the cost of the phone would be reimbursed so Garrett could get a new one. If the screen repair quote was cheaper than the cost of the phone, then the insurance company would pay for the screen repair instead. As it turned out, the screen repair was less expensive than the cost of the phone and before Garrett knew it, he had his phone repaired at no additional cost to him.

Now, about those close calls:

Theft attempt #1

The first time someone tried to steal from me was about a year into my trip (372 days to be exact) when I was in Brussels with three friends. It was my last night in Europe before flying to Colombia, and we were celebrating my friend's recent marriage. After a few delicious beers at a local bar, we were heading back to our Airbnb and were approached by two younger men. We initially thought that they were simply friendly drunks as their speech was a little bit slurred and they seemed quite jovial. One of the men put his arm around me and started jumping happily up and down. I then felt my front right pocket get rubbed. I immediately touched the front and back pockets of my jeans and realized that my phone was gone, even though I literally had it five seconds ago. Luckily, because I realized what happened so quickly, the guy still had his arm around me and I was able to grab him by the shirt and back him into a corner. I started demanding, "where is my fucking phone, give me my phone!" while he kept replying "I don't have it, I don't have it." I exclaimed, "I had it five seconds ago, give me my fucking phone!" and he seemed to realize that this situation would not end well for him. There were four of us and only two of them, not to mention that we were all bigger than they were. My stolen phone "magically" appeared in his hand. He handed my phone back to me, I made sure that my friends had all of their belongings, and we let the two men go. Later, my friend told me that he saw the thief pull my stolen phone out of his sock. Looking back on the attempted theft, I'm amazed at how quickly thefts can happen. In this situation, I was particularly lucky. I was with three friends, the thieves were smaller individuals, and no one had any weapons. This will not be the case in every bad travel situation. So be aware of your surroundings, and err on the side of safety.

Theft attempt #2

Now flash forward three days from my Brussels brush with thievery. This time I was in Colombia. It was 5 p.m. in a central area of Medellin, and I was doing a little shopping with a local Colombian woman named Andrea. When we had finished shopping and were about to part ways, she asked me if I would like her to accompany me to the metro station. I laughed at the idea in my head for a few reasons:

A) I was only three blocks away from the metro station;

B) She was a non-threatening looking woman standing at about 5'3" and couldn't have weighed more than 100 pounds;

C) The area was extremely busy with lots of people.

With these thoughts boosting my confidence, I naively assure her with a smile, "I have been traveling for over a year now, I think I will be okay." I walked one block and arrived at the intersection. As I was waiting to cross with a group of locals, I pulled out my phone to kill the time.

When the light changed, I put my phone back into my pocket and crossed the street. It was then that a local-looking man approached me and started asking for directions. From the very beginning, the situation felt suspicious to me because this man approached me (clearly a tourist), instead of other people who were also waiting at the light. While our conversation happened in Spanish, here I will translate it to English:

Man: Do you know where Park San Antonio is?

Me: Sorry, I do not know.

Man: (he repeats) Do you know where Park San Antonio is?

Me: I do not know, I do not know.

Man: You have a phone with maps, pull it out to show me where Park San Antonio is.

Me: No, no, no, sorry, I do not know!

At this point, it started to feel even more sketchy, and I quickened my walking pace.

Man: Do you want to die? (and this is where he reveals a knife from within his jacket).

Me: No, no, no, okay, okay, okay, here.

I do a quick assessment of the guy. He was probably about 40-years-old, wearing jeans, and he had a little beer belly. Meanwhile, I was wearing shorts, in decent shape, and currently standing about two feet away from him. I decided I was faster than him, so I immediately changed directions and sprinted away. He did not immediately chase me, and I darted across the street, noticing out of the corner of my eye that he also crossed the street, trying to keep tabs on me. I then lost him in a crowd of people and doubled back to the side of the street where I originally was. I then hurried to the metro station, constantly darting my eyes in all directions to ensure I did not spot him again. I do not think I took a breath the whole way to the metro station, and it wasn't until I finally got through security that I was able to relax a little bit, breathe, and calm down. It was probably one of the scariest moments of my life, but reflecting back on it, I do believe that it could happen anywhere and to anyone. People get robbed all the time in places like New York City or Chicago. Just because it happened to occur in Colombia, I did not let it negatively impact my opinion on the country as a whole. In hindsight, it may have been smarter and safer just to let the thief have my phone and utilize my travel insurance, but in the heat of the moment, I made a different split decision. Thankfully, those were the only two robbery attempts for the duration of the trip, and nothing else truly bad happened.

Section 3.11: Staying safe

Here are some techniques to keep in mind to be as safe as possible when traveling the world. You will probably realize from the stories I have told already that I do not follow these suggestions 100%, as sometimes things can be very situationally dependent. For example, when the guy tried to rob me with a knife, I thought with very high certainty that I could outrun him. If he was a younger/healthier guy, was close enough to grab me, or brandished a gun instead of a knife, of course I would have not tried to escape, and I would have given him my belongings instead.

Do not get too drunk: This should be pretty obvious, especially when you are in a foreign country, but it is still worth saying. When you are intoxicated, all of your senses are dulled, and it will be easier for people to take advantage of you.

Do not flaunt fancy jewelry: Wearing expensive or expensive-looking jewelry may serve as an advertisement to thieves that you are worth robbing. Personally, I enjoy wearing a nice watch when I go out for the evening, but when the night ends, and I need to get home, I am always sure to take the watch off and secure it out of sight before heading back out into public areas.

Do not walk home alone at night: It's true that there is safety in numbers, whether it is the friends you have been traveling with or fellow hostel travelers you met earlier in the day. However, if you do find yourself walking home alone, try to find a couple walking the same direction as you, pass them, then slow down so you are walking the same pace as them but just slightly ahead of them. This might sound absurd, but being tangentially close to other people reduces your chance of someone trying to single you out as a target. Of course this assumes that the couple does not rob you, in which case, refer back to the default rule of always being aware of your surroundings.

Do not hail a taxi from the street: Instead, always use a phone application to call the taxi. When you arrive in a country, figure out which app is most common, as there are tons of them, and sometimes it is country-dependent (Uber, Tappsi, Easy Taxi, Y.Taxi, etc.). Using an app is safer because you know the ride is coming from a verified source, and documentation of you hiring the driver increases accountability. If you hire a taxi off the street this won't be the case, and you may even be getting into a random scammer's car! An additional benefit to using a phone application instead of a street taxi is you will reduce your chance of being scammed because the price for the fare is predetermined ahead of time with the application.

Keep your money spread out in separate pockets: A thief will probably want to flee the scene of the crime as quickly as possible and, therefore, will not do a thorough search through all of your pockets. So if you are in a country where you think your chance of robbery is higher, keep a small amount of money in a second wallet. Then, if someone tries to rob you, give up your second wallet instead of your primary one.

Do not ever leave your drinks unattended: This goes

for both men and women. Also, do not accept drinks from anyone you do not know if you did not see the beverage poured. Otherwise, you run the risk of having the next thing you might remember be waking up in some random street or hospital without your wallet or phone - or worse. Really, it is safer to just buy your own drinks. In most of the countries I have visited, drinks are around $1-2, so it is not like it will break the bank, and it could save your money, valuables, or life.

Do not escalate a robbery situation: I know I am a hypocrite here, but more times than not it is smarter and safer to let the robber take your things than flee or fight. Things are replaceable (especially with the travel insurance I recommend), your life is not.

Section 3.12: Keeping your money secure

When you have scrimped and saved enough money that will allow you to travel, the last thing you want to have happen is have your hard-earned travel fund be compromised in any way. For instance, before traveling I read some pretty bad horror stories where tourists would be kidnapped and then forced to go from ATM to ATM withdrawing all the money from their checking account. While most banks nowadays will return any money that was stolen from you in the case of theft, the process can take weeks or even months to get straightened out. This can be detrimental if you are in the middle of a trip and become stranded in a city because of the theft. Lucky for you, and me, I come from a cyber security background and have developed a cyber security solution I have found to be effective while traveling. It is important to know that any security solution will never be 100% effective, but taking the following steps should help mitigate financial fallout.

Using a VPN

It is worth noting that when you connect to public Wi-Fi networks, it might be *possible* for a bad-intentioned person to hijack some of your private information, such as passwords. Therefore, it is typically ill-advised to do any sort of financial transactions (banking/purchases/credit cards) while connected to a public Wi-Fi network. However, if you are traveling for an extended period of time, there will be instances when you need to login to certain sensitive accounts with only public Wi-Fi networks available. This is where you should use a VPN. A VPN stands for *virtual private network*, and allows you to easily set up a connection to a remote server you trust, so that you can do financial transactions while connected to public Wi-Fi and not worry about your private information being compromised. Using a VPN has become incredibly simple over the past few years. There are lots of apps out there that will provide the service for free or for a small fee, for both mobile and laptop use. Paying for a VPN definitely does not have to cause a big hole in your travel budget. For instance, my VPN app costs me $20 a year, so less than $2 a month. The simple workflow is: connect to the VPN app on your phone, do whatever banking and credit card stuff you need to do, then disconnect from the VPN app. One thing to note, using a VPN will most likely slow down your connection speeds. While it is possible to have your phone be connected to the VPN app at all times (if you want maximum security), you will probably notice a slight slow-down of any other apps that use the internet. For this reason, I only use my VPN app when I am doing high security things like banking and credit card transactions.

Investigate the ATM

Criminals have gotten pretty crafty over the years when it comes to trying to steal your debit card information during an ATM transaction. When selecting an ATM to withdraw money from, a general rule-of-thumb is to pick an ATM located in a bank. These ATMs are more closely watched and, thus, have a lower probability of being tampered. However, regardless of where the ATM is, **always** inspect the slot where you insert your card beforehand. Make sure there are no loose pieces or added components, as many times a criminal will add a device which basically steals your debit card number. Next, always cover your typing hand with your other hand when you are entering your PIN. Sometimes criminals will install little cameras over the keypad which will record you typing in your PIN; covering your typing hand will thwart this scheme. Following these rules will help prevent your debit card information from being stolen whenever you are withdrawing money.

My financial pipeline

Finally, I was a little worried about the aforementioned scenario of being abducted and having all of the money drained out of my checking account. Therefore, I developed a system that would help protect me from the unlikely scenario in addition to protecting me if my debit card information was stolen. First, I had my main bank account, which had all of the money I saved up for traveling the world. There is no debit card associated with my main account, so that banking information will never get stolen from a compromised ATM. Next, I opened two additional checking accounts with debit cards, where one debit card was my primary card which I use for day-to-day ATM withdrawals, and the second debit card was my backup card, which I kept hidden in my backpack. If somehow my primary debit card's information was stolen (which, unfortunately, has happened throughout the trip), I am able to switch to my backup card and use that one until I can get my primary debit card replaced. As you can see, having a backup card can help prevent you from being stranded in case of a hacked card. From my checking accounts, I can do cash transfers from my main bank account to ensure my debit cards always have money (I would keep my primary card topped up around $500 and my backup card around $250). The benefits of this are twofold. First, because I am doing cash transfers from my checking accounts, I never have to login to my main bank account online. This helps prevent my main bank account from ever getting compromised. Next, keeping the maximum amounts on my debit cards at any given time relatively low gives me some assurance that if I was ever abducted and forced to withdraw money from my debit card, the absolute maximum amount the criminal could ever get would be $500.

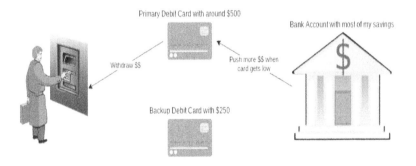

A) Normal operation of my debit cards when withdrawing money

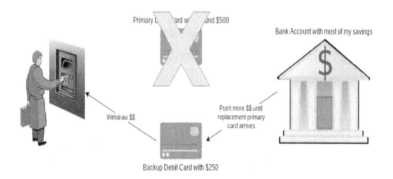

Primary Debit Card with around $500

Bank Account with most of my savings

Withdraw $$

Push more $$ until replacement primary card arrives

Backup Debit Card with $250

B) Switching to the backup card if the primary card is hacked and I need a replacement card shipped to me

Section 4: Lessons learned

"A mind that is stretched by a new experience can never go back to its old dimensions" – Oliver Wendell Holmes

My 500 days traveling the world were filled with countless priceless experiences. Through these experiences, I discovered countless things about myself, adjusted many of my behaviors, and changed my overall outlook on life. I can best summarize these discoveries in five major life lessons, which I will expand upon here.

Section 4.1: Minimalism

Coming from a capitalist country, I was raised thinking that the more things I had in my life, the happier I would be. As we grow older, this desire tends to seep into almost every aspect of our lives. Whether it be a new outfit, the latest telephone model, or that sandwich press your mother just bought you; the truth of the matter is, you probably do not need it. I was no exception to this feeling of wanting more and more things—even feeling like I somehow needed them to be happy or complete. Before traveling, my apartment was littered with impulse Amazon purchases, ranging from rarely used specialty kitchen appliances to clothes I almost never wear. I had an Air Fryer, a spiralizer, a five-blade vegetable slicer, a banana slicer, a pasta making machine, a sandwich press, and more. Why did I have all these things? Who knows. It is not like I would use them frequently. At best, I would use one kitchen appliance every few months. This compulsive consumerism also engulfed me when it came to shoes. I had 16 pairs of shoes. It used to be a goal of mine to have a pair of shoes in every color, so I could perfectly match every possible outfit. Again, why? Looking back, I can no longer reasonably justify owning 16 pairs of shoes. Maybe five pairs, tops, but that is it.

At the very start of my trip, when I deboarded my plane and stepped into Ukraine, I had a 55-liter backpacking bag strapped to my back, as well as a 35-liter backpack resting on my front. Carrying both bags simultaneously was quite heavy, but I thought I *needed* everything I had brought with me, so I pushed on. As my travels continued, I began to grow tired of carrying so much. I also did not like the double backpack look, as I thought I looked ridiculous and ultra-touristy. "Do I even need so much stuff?" I would think to myself. So at the end of month two, I decided to do my first "purge." I went through both of my bags and picked up each item one by one, questioning: "Have I used this item at all in the last month? Is there any way I can see myself using this item in the future?" If the answer was no to both questions, then the item would be placed in my purge pile. When my first purge concluded, I had managed to empty out nearly everything in my 35-liter front bag! I also felt some satisfaction as I realized that I was able to donate my unwanted clothes to other travelers or people less fortunate than myself. After this first purge, I was able to reduce my belongings to the point where I could fit my smaller bag within my larger bag, so when I was on the move I only needed to carry one bag. I cannot emphasize how much happier this made me, as now I felt more like a proper traveler, rather than a bumbling tourist.

As my travels continued, I would periodically have additional purges, usually every two months. It almost got to a point where purging became like a game in which the objective was to reduce my belongings as much as humanly possible. Every single thing I would remove resulted in less weight I needed to drag around, as well as making me feel more authentic as a traveler. My rules for purging stayed consistent: if they were not used in the last month, and I did not think I would use it in the near future, it was removed. Near the end of my trip I had reduced my clothes load to the perfect amount for me (although the urge to reduce still persisted!):

- 2 daytime t-shirts

- 2 long sleeve shirts (for sun/insect protection or hiking)
- 2 "bro-tanks"
- 4 boxers
- 3 pairs of socks
- 1 pair of basketball shorts
- 1 pair of hiking pants (the ones that zip off into shorts, super cool right?)
- 1 pair of super thin pants for sleeping
- 1 pair flip flops
- 1 pair of black walking/trekking shoes
- 2 going out shirts
- 1 pair of jeans

Even looking at this list now, it feels too long. I wish I could get rid of more, but it is difficult to reduce further without losing flexibility. For example, I kept clothes for both warmer and colder climates in order to extend my travel options both in time and place.

Extended travel also meant I had to learn how to extend the life of my minimalist wardrobe. As you can probably predict, wearing only a few outfits day-in and day-out will eventually result in tears. Imagine my dismay when I discovered that my only (and favorite) pair of jeans had ripped a good-sized hole right in the crotch! I was in Uzbekistan, and I had serious doubts about whether or not I could find a replacement pair of jeans that fit me as well as my current pair. After giving it some thought, I went out to buy black thread and a needle, watched a couple YouTube videos on beginner sewing, and went to work. About an hour later, my first ever sewing job was complete, and I must say it was not that bad! It was definitely passable and the jeans actually survived until the end of my trip. Since that first time sewing my jeans, the skill has come in handy numerous times. I was able to repair boxers, socks, pajama pants, and even a small hole in my trekking shoes!

Looking back at all the things I purchased and owned in my old life in the United States, I realized that very few of these things actually made me *happier*. Alternatively, as I traveled, I found the *less* I carried, the *less* I had, the lighter and *happier* I felt. I hope to take this lesson with me when I return to the United States. It will also be a lesson I share with other travelers, like a young Ukrainian woman I met at the beginning of my trip had shared with me. She was my Couchsurfing host, living in Odessa. She lived in a small studio apartment and owned very few possessions. After some chatting, she told me she only had five outfits: one pair of pajamas, three casual outfits, and one dress. She told me how happy she was in life and how she actually enjoys having a minimal number of outfits. She explained how she never stresses out about what she is going to wear each day. It took me awhile to understand how someone with so little could be so happy, but after traveling for some time with only a backpack, it starts to become so obviously apparent. I firmly believe if you remove the excess things from your life, those innocuous items you never use, you will partially feel "set free" and as a result live a happier and less stressful life.

Section 4.2: General kindness in people

If you only watch the news and never leave your country, you may have the mindset that the world is a scary and evil place filled with people who will either take advantage of you, rob you, or murder you. I mostly blame the news for these preconceived notions about the outside world, because broadcasts seem to only focus on the problems in the world. Because of this, I was very nervous the first time I traveled overseas. Like most people, I had grown up being constantly bombarded with reports on how dangerous other places were. It cultivates a certain frame of mind that you must always be suspicious and trust no one. This mindset stayed with me at the beginning of my travels, but I was able to shed it with experience after experience of individuals and families showing me so much generosity. There are literally so many examples from my travels it could fill a whole book in itself, so here I will only give a few:

Biking in Vietnam: One of my longtime dreams was to get a motorcycle in Vietnam and drive from the North to the South. I was blessed enough to be able to accomplish this dream during my journey with one of my best friends, Jon. After full mornings on the road, we would inevitably get hungry. Our method of finding food was to drive around whatever town we were in until we saw a restaurant or food stand with a lot of local people eating. We reasoned that if a lot of local people enjoyed this food, then it would be good enough for us as well! One day, we were driving in the middle of nowhere in Vietnam and were hungry. It was about 2 p.m., and we had not had anything to eat since breakfast much earlier. Luckily, we had just arrived at a decent-sized village so we started aimlessly driving around looking for food. Unfortunately, none of the restaurants we spotted looked very busy (likely because it was a little late in the day for lunch in Vietnam). After passing about 10 empty restaurants and starting to lose hope, we happened upon a small house. In front of the house were two long picnic tables filled with food and people engaged in lively conversation. We stopped our bikes about 100 feet away and started talking amongst ourselves. It did not look like a typical restaurant because there were no signs or other indicators. As we were debating between ourselves, a lady from one of the tables stood up, started waving her arms, and hollered, "Hey, you! Come, come!" We immediately hopped off our bikes and joined them for what would turn out to be an incredibly fun next three hours.

It turned out to be a family celebrating because one member of the family had just bought a new house in the village. No one was able to speak English, but thanks to Google Translate, we were able to communicate and share stories. There were so many different types of delicious food on the table, and they kept offering us more and more food whenever our plates would become even slightly empty. They also seemed to have an endless supply of beer, which they were more than happy to share with us. Near the end, they set up a Karaoke system, and I was able to jam out to "Don't Stop Believin'." However, what stands out the most from this memory is that we talked about some heavy topics like the Vietnam War. Because it is a relatively recent event, unfortunately most of them knew someone who died in the war. Yet what I found truly special was their ability to not hold grudges, and when we told them we were Americans, they were excited and shouted with joy. It was surreal to think about how they could display so much kindness and generosity to people from the United States when they had something so devastating happen in their country not too long ago.

Making a friend in Tajikistan: It was a beautiful morning in Dushanbe, Tajikistan, so I decided I would just relax in the main square. I was sitting and enjoying the wonderful day for about 20 minutes when a man sat next to me and began talking with me. His name was Abu, and he was a 22-year-old interested in politics and learning languages. After some nice discussion, he invited me to his family's house in the evening and said I was more than welcome to spend the night. I enthusiastically accepted, as seeing how locals actually live is an incredible experience. We swapped telephone numbers and parted ways. That evening I was walking to his house, and although it was close to the center of the city of Dushanbe, this particular neighborhood felt like a small village instead. The streets were narrow and cobblestoned, filled with children running around playing games and goats grazing on whatever foliage they could find. I arrived at his house and was warmly greeted by his grandparents, nieces, uncles, and aunts. He led me to the room where I would be staying and, to my surprise, in the middle of the room there was a table loaded with delicious snacks. This table had everything: tea, baked goods, strawberries, cherries, almonds, peanuts, cashews, and chocolates! But what really blew me away was that I learned that during the day, Abu went out and bought all these treats just for me, purely out of kindness. I should mention that I visited him during Ramadan, which is a religious period for Muslims where they fast during the day. I felt bad because he was not allowed to eat at this time, but he reassured me that it was okay for me to eat in front of him, so I helped myself to the delicious food as we talked. He explained that in his culture, it was expected to treat guests with the utmost respect and care. This level of hospitality was something I had not experienced before, and I was overwhelmed by what lengths Abu and his family would go through during my stay to ensure that I was comfortable.

Trains in India: I always seemed to meet the nicest people when I was riding on trains in India. I do not know if I perpetually looked hungry during this portion of my trip, but Indians would almost always offer to share their food with me while I was on the train. One time, I was riding the train on my way to Jodhpur, trying to work on my laptop, when a nice older gentleman started talking to me. His name was Anil, and he had a background in IT, so we immediately clicked and chatted off and on for the remainder of the train ride. It was a little late (around 9 p.m.) when we arrived in Jodhpur, when Anil told me that he owned a restaurant/bakery in the area and was wondering if I would like to come and try some local Indian foods. As if the offer was not amazing enough already, he even had a driver waiting at the train station so we could simply hop in and go. Obviously I said, "of course!" so we got in his car and headed to his restaurant. When we arrived, he talked briefly with one of his employees and then started ordering pretty much everything on the menu! We ate Kachori (fried dumplings), Samosas, Pani Puri, and much more. When my stomach felt like it was about to explode, the waiter brought out freshly baked sweets (Kaju Katali). All the food was delicious, but at this point I was so full. I felt like I had eaten three meals, and I had to tell Anil I simply could not eat anymore. He smiled and laughed, saying "no problem" while he continued to order me more and more food. Thankfully, when the new food came, he put it all in a to-go bag for me. In total, the to-go bag probably weighed around 5 pounds and was more than enough food to last me the next 3 days in Jodhpur.

After seeing strangers demonstrate so much kindness towards me, it really made me reflect on some of the preconceived notions I held. My experiences have taught me that most of the world is not as bad or dangerous of a place as it is made out to be. Sure, some countries are unfortunately riddled with violence due to political or religious extremism, but that is simply not what I experienced. By and large, if I met a random person in the street in any of the countries I visited, the person was extremely kind, wished only the best for me, and often would even try to help me in any way they could. Of course, that cannot be not true for every single person you could possibly meet, but I found it was generally true. The only group of people that I found consistent in their efforts to try and rip me off, no matter which country I was in, were taxi drivers (sorry but not sorry to any taxi drivers reading this). Whenever a taxi driver knew I was a foreigner, he (also consistent, all my taxi drivers were men) would try to rip me off in one way or another, either by not running the meter, quoting me an absurd price, or setting the meter to some "premium" mode. After experiencing this time and time again, I started to avoid taxis at all costs because I knew it would end in an argument or with me getting ripped off. That exception aside, literally every other group of people I came across were incredibly warm and kind. The world is filled with individuals who are proud of their country and want to ensure travelers have a fantastic time when visiting. I plan to take this lesson back to the United States with me and apply it in my day to day life. If I see anyone who looks like they are lost or confused tourists, I will approach them and try to help them to the best of my ability. After all, I now feel certain that, if the roles were reversed and I were lost or confused in their country, they would most definitely lend a helping hand to me.

Section 4.3: Luck for where I was born

One of the most humbling lessons I learned while traveling abroad is just how lucky I was to be born to a middle-class family in the United States. Growing up, it was really easy to be shortsighted and naive. When I was a child, I remember walking up and down the soybean fields of my family's farm, picking weeds with my brothers. I found the work to be mind-numbingly boring, and to make matters worse, we had to do this in the peak of summer heat in rural Illinois. I hated doing this, and I remember thinking it was incredibly unfair. I did not see my friends and classmates doing this, so why did I have to? But in reality, this minimal amount of work pales in comparison to what other children across the world go through. Up until this point, it had been so easy to take all of the advantages I have for granted because I had nothing else with which to compare. However, seeing the lack of opportunity and hardships that people go through every day in other places really made me realize how lucky I am. Even the fact that you, dear reader, can so much as read this book means that you are more educated and likely better off than many people throughout the world. This realization became extremely apparent to me during my Workaway in Thailand. If you recall, I was teaching English in a small village. As you would expect with any class, some children were under-achievers, while others really did try hard to learn. Five of the children I taught in particular were extremely bright. They were very quick learners and could retain information much quicker than the rest of the class.

To my dismay, I learned that all five of these kids were immigrants from Myanmar and did not have any sort of citizenship. In Thailand, this means they will never be able to attend a university or obtain higher education. This realization left me distraught. If these children were born in the United States, they would be enrolled in Honors classes, excelling in school, and most likely be granted the opportunity to attend a university when they were older. They could be future doctors, engineers, lawyers, or anything else their hearts desired. Instead, the harsh reality was that they seem doomed to remain in the same small village for the rest of their lives, working in the tea fields day in and day out. How can something that seems so ruthlessly arbitrary as where you are born have such a damaging impact on a young bright mind? This certainly made me reflect on my own life. With all else equal, if I had been born in this village instead of the United States, I do not think I would ever have been able to do what I am doing now. I would not be able to get a proper education or land a decent job, let alone travel the world.

Another thing I took for granted before I started traveling is how powerful the United States passport is. As an American, I can travel to every country in Europe without needing a visa beforehand. Likewise, in South America, most countries will give Americans 90 "free" days upon arrival. While I did need a visa to visit many places in Asia, they were typically E-Visas and I could complete it online by filling out a simple form and paying a small sum, usually between $20-40. I soon came to realize that this ease of travel is not the same for citizens of all other countries. In Turkey, I was staying with this awesome Couchsurfing host named Bruno, who was pretty much the embodiment of everything good in the Couchsurfing culture. Every night, he would host multiple people (usually 8+) from all around the world, and we would come together to share stories and laughter over a home-cooked meal. It was there where I met two friendly Iranian men. After talking with them for awhile, it dawned on me just how easy I had it traveling around with a passport from the United States. They explained to me that they were in Turkey because it was pretty much the only country they could visit that is close to Iran and visa-free. You can look at the map below which depicts where Iranians can go visa-free (dark green). Everywhere in gray they need a visa (and not an e-visa).

Where Iranians can go based on color (from

https://en.wikipedia.org/wiki/Visa_requirements_for_Iran
ian_citizens)

For most of the countries they wish to visit, it is not a simple online visa application like it is for Americans. Instead, they need to physically go to an embassy with their passport, photos, application visa, proof of enough money in the bank, travel itinerary (sometimes), fingerprints, and more. It usually takes me about one to three days to get an e-visa. For an Iranian, the minimum is usually 15 days. This was terrible for my two Iranian friends who just wanted to see the world. They have the same travel dreams and desires as me, but their path to do so is filled with an exorbitant number of roadblocks, solely because of where they happen to have been born.

Section 4.4: Go with the flow

Before taking this trip, I would describe myself as a pretty impatient person. If an elevator took longer than a minute to come, I would say screw it and take the stairs. Or I would get agitated when people were standing on both the left and right side of escalators, preventing others from walking up them. However, my travels forced me to change this aspect of myself. In many parts of the world, life moves a little—or a lot!—differently than it does in the United States. For example, in many parts of Central Asia, the main mode of transportation is via a Marshrutka. A Marshrutka is basically an old van, similar to a bus, but it will only leave for its destination when it is completely full of passengers. To make things even more frustrating, if you are in a more remote area, Marshrutkas would only run once or twice a week. If you miss one, you are simply out of luck for a couple days. There were times I found myself waiting more than four hours in a Marshrutka, just so it could fill with people and finally depart. I am sure if the old, impatient me had been in this situation, I would have gone insane by hour two Luckily at this point I had learned another super important lesson of traveling: go with the flow.

All of my trips before this one had been short, usually around two weeks. Because of the limited timeline, I usually planned out most of my itinerary beforehand because I wanted to see as many regions and attractions of the country as possible. The problem with this system is that if something goes wrong, like a delayed or cancelled flight, bus, or train, it could wreak havoc on your planned itinerary. When I initially started my journey in Ukraine, I attempted to continue using this planned itinerary method. I would over plan things and stress out if a bus or train was late. After some time, I realized the error in my approach. Since I was not on a tight timeline anymore, I could just go with the flow and see where the journey takes me. This realization allowed me to shed a lot of stress that had previously burdened me, stress that I had essentially brought on myself. A train is cancelled? Who cares, I will take the next one. A hostel is fully-booked? Who cares, I will walk to the next one. Furthermore, this "go with the flow" attitude allowed me to experience things I do not think would have been possible otherwise. This open schedule allowed me to be extremely fluid. If I met interesting travelers who were going somewhere that sounded fun, I could simply join them. If someone told me about an amazing place I had not originally planned on visiting, I could simply change my plans and explore this new place.

Probably the best example demonstrating the benefits of going with the flow was when this flexibility allowed me to visit the wonderful country of Georgia. Within my first two weeks of traveling throughout Ukraine, I had more than 10 people tell me something along the lines of, "You need to go to Georgia, it is absolutely beautiful and amazing!" Being the ignorant American that I was, up until this point I had never even heard of the country Georgia, let alone considered going there. But after hearing about how great it was for the tenth time, I decided, "Okay, now I have to go there!" When I eventually went, I had an absolute blast. The food was delicious and cheap, the people were friendly (and could usually speak English), and it was one of the easiest countries to hitchhike in that I had visited. Looking back, if my schedule had been as rigid as it used to be, I would have never been able to visit that wonderful country. When I am back in the United States, I hope to continue this "go with the flow" attitude and not allow my impatient attitude to return and get the best of me. I have learned that holding on to this rigid schedule and impatient mindset just adds unnecessary stress, which is not something anyone needs more of in their lives.

Section 4.5: Being outgoing

If you are anything like me, it might be difficult for you to be outgoing and start talking to random strangers. While I do gain some "liquid courage" when I have been drinking, when I am sober it can be a very different story. At the beginning of my travels, I would feel social anxiety, which prevented me from talking to people on buses or trains. However, over time, I learned that even the tiniest effort towards being outgoing can lead to amazing interactions with people you would not have had otherwise. I found that something as simple as, "Hey, how is it going?" with a smile can do wonders. If the person is not interested in chatting, he or she will give a short response. It is important to not take this personally or get down on yourself. I realized that if I do not attempt to talk to a person I am sitting next to on the bus or plane, I am actually doing myself a disservice in the sense of a missed opportunity or a conversation with someone interesting. Here is an example of how the simple act of being friendly can go a long way:

It was midnight as I anxiously waited to board my plane to leave Uzbekistan. I needed to leave the country immediately, as it was the last day of my visa, and I did not want to find out what would happen to me if I overstayed my welcome. The night ahead of me would be less than thrilling because I would land in Dushanbe, Tajikistan around 2 a.m., but my Couchsurfing host would not be awake to meet me until around 7 a.m. This left me with about five hours of down time, which I planned to spend trying to rest on an uncomfortable bench or floor in the airport lobby of Dushanbe. Thankfully, the potentially dreary night had a much better ending. As I boarded the plane, I sat down and glanced at the guy next to me. He had short blonde hair, glasses, blue eyes, and a stockier build. He certainly did not look like a typical Uzbekistan person, and although it was already late and I was tired, I decided to try chatting with him a little bit. His name was Eugene, and as luck would have it, he turned out to also be an American. We ended up deep in conversation for the entire plane ride, as he regaled me with stories about his awesome job. His title was "World Price Consultant," and let me tell you, it sounds like a job I would love to have. Basically, for four months of every year, his company sends him to various parts of the world in order to talk to clients and catalogue the cost of living in a particular city or country. His company puts him up in nice hotels, pays for his meals, and sends him to a bunch of exotic places—sounds like a travelers dream to me! When our plane landed in Dushanbe, I was about to say goodbye when he offered to let me sleep on his couch in his hotel room. Obviously a couch sounded better than whatever bench I would end up on at the airport, so I graciously accepted and off we went. For the next four days I had a free hotel to stay at, and, when he was not working, we explored the city, drank beers, and genuinely had a good time.

Looking back on the experience, I am grateful I had the courage to go out on a limb and spark a conversation with a stranger on the plane. Not only did the simple action result in me getting a free place to stay for four days with an incredibly awesome breakfast, but more importantly, it allowed me to meet and become good friends with someone who would otherwise be a total stranger. If I had decided I was too tired or too shy to make the attempt, I would have never had the opportunity to befriend such a nice guy.

A similar experience occurred when I arrived at the bus station in Baku, Azerbaijan. It was one of those days where social anxiety was getting the best of me, and I felt like I simply did not have the energy to meet new people. I had just purchased a Kebab and selected an empty table to sit at when I overheard a conversation in English going on at the table behind me. It was an American woman speaking with an Australian woman about the current political climate in the United States. I listened nervously for awhile, wondering if I should say something. No, I kept telling myself, my lack of confidence besting me. It was at this point the American woman said something I massively disagreed with, and I thought to myself, "shit, now I need to jump in", so I turned around, introduced myself, and joined the conversation. The conversation slowly turned to other things, and as luck would have it, in an hour we would all be on the same bus! The American woman's name was Mary, and she lived in NYC. We chatted off and on throughout the bus ride and actually ended up traveling together in Azerbaijan and Georgia for the next two weeks. During those two weeks, we had some fantastic times hitchhiking, meeting locals, and getting wine drunk. I am very grateful to have met her because we went to some pretty remote areas where we did not see any other tourists, and it was better to share the experience with someone else.

My travels were filled with countless experiences similar to these two examples. I would find myself alone, begin to feel a little lonely, and in turn this loneliness would force me to be more outgoing than I had previously been. Looking forward, I hope to keep this lesson with me in my heart and continue to make efforts to be more outgoing in my day to day life.

Section 5: Go and travel!

"Travel isn't always pretty. It isn't always comfortable. Sometimes it hurts, it even breaks your heart. But that's okay. The journey changes you; it should change you. It leaves marks on your memory, on your consciousness, on your heart, and on your body. You take something with you. Hopefully, you leave something good behind." –
Anthony Bourdain

This is the end of the book; I hope you feel inspired to see the world! Remember, travel does not have to be some hugely expensive or overly complex ordeal. In fact, it should be the opposite. If a family wants to have food with you, graciously accept. Do not be above sleeping on someone's couch because it will give you a totally different perspective on how people in different parts of the world live. Partake in hitchhiking once in a while. The people who stop for you will be super interesting and only want the best for you. Get out of your comfort zone and talk to strangers in order to learn about their cultures and share your own. You will be surprised how something as innocuous as taking a public bus or train can be filled with so many incredible moments if you just make a little effort to be friendly. So take that trip and embark on that journey. You will not regret it, and you will learn more about yourself and others than you probably thought possible.

Appendix: Essential travel items

If you have made it this far in the book, I can only assume you are a traveler or traveler-to-be. To make your journey easier, here I recommend the best things I carried with me. While some of these travel products or apps are pretty obvious and can be found on many lists online, a few are not, so please do not skip over this section! I do not receive any money for suggesting or endorsing any particular brands or products. I choose to support these items because I have used them personally, and they are simply amazing.

Must have travel products

Quick dry towel: As you might suspect, this towel dries really fast! As a traveler, you are constantly moving around from place to place, and if you pack a wet towel it will quickly acquire that terrible damp, musty smell. My quick dry towel usually dries in under an hour, so it is ideal for traveling. It is also super thin and compact, so it will be a space saver in your bag. The only downside is that it will not get you as completely dry as its cotton towel counterpart, but it is definitely sufficient. There are tons of brands out there that come in various shapes and sizes, so you can pick out what suits you best.

Travel debit card: I think a good travel debit card is the most important thing on this list. By now you have learned carrying lots of cash with you is silly and only opens you up for a world of hurt if you are the unfortunate victim of theft.

This pain can be mitigated with a good travel debit card. The one that I love is Charles Schwab High Yield Investor Checking Account. I love this card so much I travel with two, one as my primary and one as a backup. The card includes similar benefits as other travel cards such as fraud protection (which protects you if you get hacked), and 0% foreign transaction fees. However, the real perk that makes this card go from great to outstanding is the monthly ATM rebate. You know those pesky fees you get charged when you withdraw money from a bank which is not your own bank? At the end of every month, this card refunds those fees back to your account! Think about how incredible that is for a second. Every time you withdraw money from your account you will never pay ATM fees! You need to have a card like this when you travel.

Travel credit card: While most of the places I visited on my journey were places where credit cards were not really utilized, it was still nice to have a credit card to pay for visa applications and other online transactions. It was also particularly handy to have a credit card in the few countries where credit cards dominated the market. There are so many credit cards out there, it should not be hard to find one for which you qualify. The one big requirement to look for is a card that has 0% foreign transaction fees. If you do not get a card with this, the usual fee is 3%, which definitely would add up over a long period of time traveling in a country that uses credit cards. The other nice thing to look for in a travel card is something with low or 0% cash advance fees. Keep in mind, using a credit card for a cash advance should only be used *in the most serious of emergencies*, otherwise, use your travel debit card for cash.

LifeStraw: A LifeStraw is essentially a filter that removes all of the bacteria and sediment from the water you place it in. To use, simply place it halfway in the water source you want to drink from, wait five seconds, then start to suck through the straw. Easy, right? The filter even has a lifespan of 1000 gallons (4000 liters), so if you drink an average amount of water a day it will last you three to four years before needing a new one! While there are other water cleansing solutions out there, they all have drawbacks which the LifeStraw does not. For instance, with water purification tablets, you have to wait about 30 minutes before you are able to drink the water. While waiting 30 minutes will most likely not result in a life or death situation, it is definitely an inconvenience. There is also a pen (SteriPen) that shines an ultraviolet light into the water, and it becomes clean. The issues with this device is it does not filter out elements, as well as requires batteries or maintaining a charge, both potentially problematic if you are doing multi-day hikes or in remote areas where power is limited. The LifeStraw is a fast, convenient option to stay hydrated. As I am writing this sentence I am drinking water I just gathered from a random river in India through my LifeStraw. So yes, I think it is an incredible product to be added to every traveler's repertoire.

Portable battery: You probably already have a portable battery, but if you do not, please get one. You can use them to charge your devices when there are no outlets available. A portable battery is particularly useful when you are out and about all day, on long train or bus rides, on multi-day hikes, or any other situation where you will not be next to a power outlet for some time. Portable batteries come in all sizes, from ridiculously tiny to obnoxiously gargantuan. Generally, the different sizes equate with how much charge the portable battery will be able to hold. The one I used is 13000mAh, and is able to charge my phone from 0-100% battery three times before the portable battery needs to be recharged. Get a size which you think will best fit your needs.

Travel backpack: Having a travel backpack should go without saying, but I will include it just in case. I can promise that if you bring a rolling suitcase, you will regret it. You will grow tired of rolling a suitcase around by the second week. Instead, get a proper travel backpack. Not only will it be easier to move around, but you will also look much less like a tourist. My travel backpack's size is 55L; this is good for me because I do a bit of hiking and multi day treks. For most people, however, a 45L backpack should be more than enough. Always consider, the bigger the bag, the more weight you are likely to carry. I know because this is what I did when I started my trip.

Small & collapsible day bag / weekend bag: This is critical because, when you leave your hostel for the day to go exploring, you do not want to carry your travel backpack. Instead, bring a smaller bag that fits your needs for the day. For example, when exploring a new city, I usually carried a day bag containing a water bottle, sunglasses, hat, sunscreen, snacks, and passport. I found that a 20L bag was the perfect size for me. You want it to be collapsible because when you are moving between cities you can fold it up and put it inside your main pack. When I originally started my journey, I had a day bag with a frame, which I quickly realized it did not work for my travel style. Every time I had to move between cities I had to have my large bag on my back with another bag on my chest. It was not fun, especially when trying to board a full bus or metro! The other perk of my 20L bag is that it easily functions as a pack that can last me with two or three days worth of clothes. This allows me to leave my big and heavy pack in a main city, go explore a different area for a few days, then return and collect the big pack. You do not know how much of a relief you will feel for those three days only carrying your small bag!

Sleep headphones: Imagine a sleeping mask and earbuds rolled into one, and that is what you get with sleep headphones. Flat headphones are imbedded into the headband of the sleeping mask, allowing you to listen to music or white noise while you sleep. Because the headphones are flat, you can sleep on your side without ear irritation. Initially, I was wary of hostels because I am a light sleeper and need the room to be dark with some sort of background noise (like a fan), while not having other noise (like doors constantly opening and closing). To make matters worse, I tend to sleep on my side, so it is uncomfortable to sleep with earbuds in my ear. This product covered my eyes to allow it to be dark and has these flat earbuds built into the headband that can play music into my ear! I think it is the perfect device for those with similar sleeping needs to be able to fall asleep in hostels where there are no guarantees of darkness or quiet. There are many different brands, some with Bluetooth and others that connect directly to your phone. While the Bluetooth ones are great because you do not have to worry about cables, it is another device you will need to charge. An alternative to this would be a combination of a sleeping mask and earplugs.

Universal outlet adapter: There are 15 different wall outlet plug types in the world today, so if you are going to be a global traveler, you definitely do not want to be carrying lots of adapters around all of the time. Instead, get a universal outlet adapter, which will allow you to plug in successfully to nearly every country in the world. Lots of people ask if they need a voltage converter as well, and the answer is typically no. Most modern devices can handle a range of voltages as input without a problem. Simply look at the electronic devices you plan on bringing on your trip, and if they say "input: 100-240V," then you are okay.

Spin Lock: Most hostels have lockers where you can store your most precious valuables (passport, credit/debit cards, laptops) as long as you bring your own lock. So invest in a good one, but make sure the band is not too thick or it will not fit in the holes of some of the lockers.

Unlocked phone: If you are going to be traveling abroad and want to use local SIM cards, make sure your phone is unlocked before you leave on your trip. This is usually as simple as calling your provider and asking them to unlock it.

Amazing travel applications

Google Maps: I used this application to download offline maps for the cities I visited. Once I have the offline version downloaded, I can easily navigate between places using GPS instead of relying on a Wi-Fi or data connection.

MAPS.ME: This is another navigation app. I found MAPS.ME is not as useful as Google Maps when traveling in cities. Where it really flourishes is when trekking, as this application has significantly more hiking trails than its Google Maps counterpart. It also provides offline maps, so you won't need a connection in the middle of the mountains.

Google Translate: Two things make Google Translate special. First, you can download offline language packages for offline translation. Second, if you do have a Wi-Fi connection you can use conversation mode. When in this mode, you simply talk into the phone, and the app will translate into the other language and speak it aloud. Then the other person can speak his or her language, and it will translate it back to English. Thanks to this app, I was able to have an interesting conversation for hours with a Vietnamese man, even though I could not speak any Vietnamese, and he could not speak any English!

A VPN app: A VPN app will help make sure your banking or credit card transactions remain secure when you are connected to potentially malicious Wi-Fi networks overseas. With a VPN app, all you do is start the connection, use whatever apps or websites you want to use, then disconnect from the app. Most of the VPN apps available are super simple to use, but be aware, if you use the VPN on at all times website will load a little slower, which is why I recommend only using it when you are doing something that should be truly secure.

WhatsApp: WhatsApp is a lightweight chat application which allows you to send messages, make voice calls, or perform video chat. When traveling, you will find this is the most common application both locals and other travelers use to stay in contact with one another, so it is best to have it downloaded. One thing to be aware of is that each country has a specific country code. For example, the United States' country code is +1, while India's is +91. When you are creating a contact for a new friend you just made, make sure you include the country code in the number, or else you will not be able to message the person on WhatsApp.

Booking.com: Throughout my time traveling, I have used many different apps to book hostels or homestays, but booking.com became my favorite one. I have found that it has more places than other applications, and if you use the application frequently you start getting a "Genius %" discount. With this discount, my accommodation is almost always a little cheaper than if I were to get it through a different app. Another bonus with booking.com is you rarely have to make a deposit; instead, you pay the entire thing when you get to the hostel. This prevents you from needing to input a credit or debit card every time. Finally, I found the cancellation policy to usually be generous. I could make a cancellation the day of my reservation and not be penalized.

Hostelworld: After booking.com, this is my next favorite app to find a hostel for the night. Some downsides are you do have to pay a deposit up front when you make a reservation, and the cancellation policy is a little stricter than booking.com. However, as a benefit I usually find more travelers use Hostelworld, so if I want to find out where other people will most likely be, then Hostelworld will be able to provide that information. It even gives you some basic demographic information, like the average age of people who stay at the hostel, so you can get an expectation for the type of people staying at the hostel with you.

Contact

I hope you had as much fun reading *Work, Save, Travel, Repeat* as I had writing it. If you have any suggestions, questions, thoughts, anything at all—please do not hesitate to reach out to me! I plan on updating the book in response to reader's input.

Email: jereme.lamps@gmail.com

Instagram: jereme.lamps

(my old handle @jersgonewhere was hacked)

Jereme M. Lamps

Made in the USA
Las Vegas, NV
16 March 2023

69191431R00100